THE PICTURE BO

GOLF

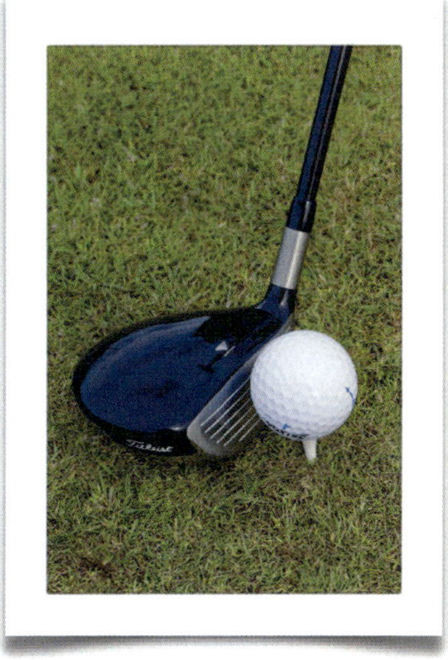

SUNNY STREET
BOOKS

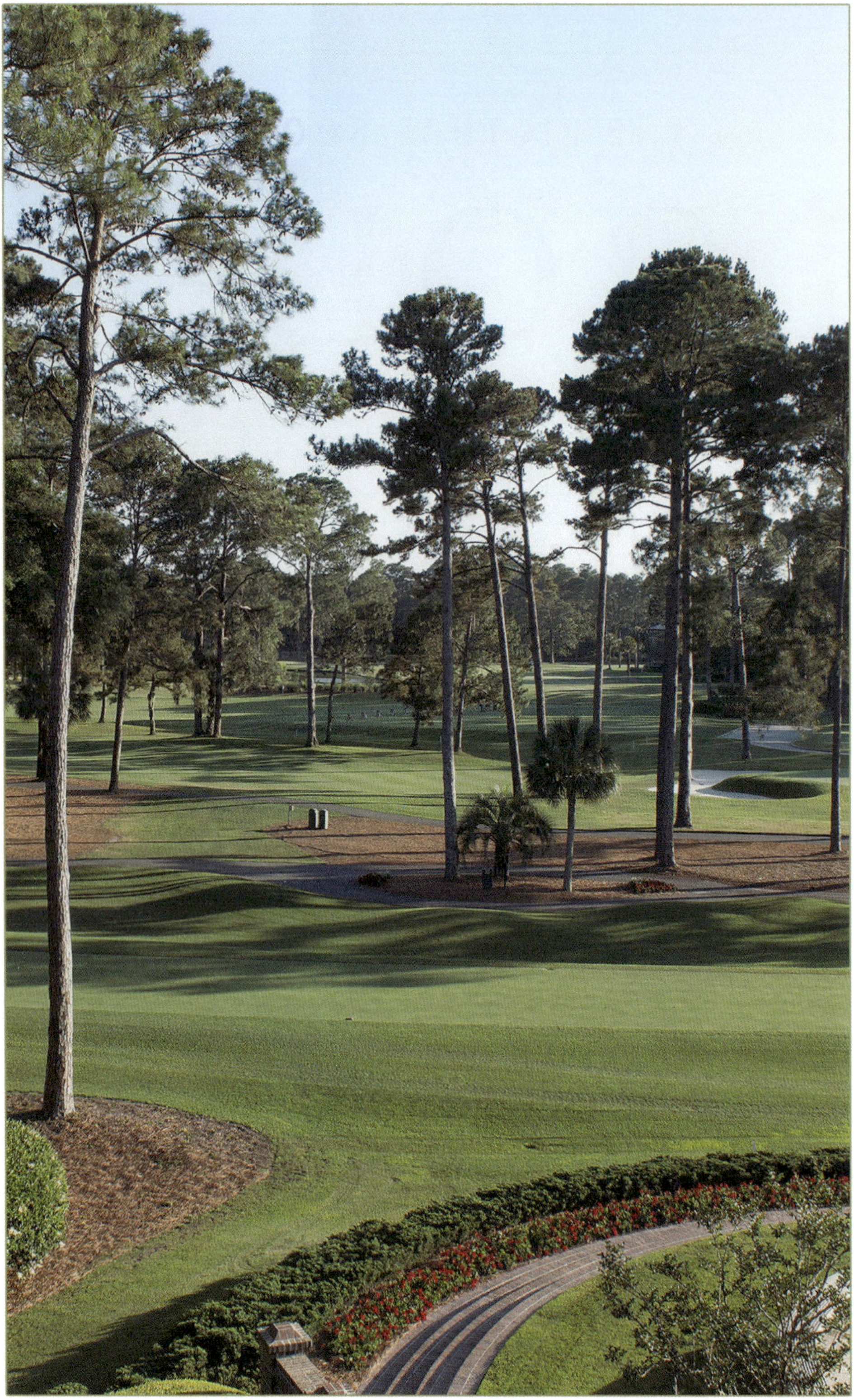

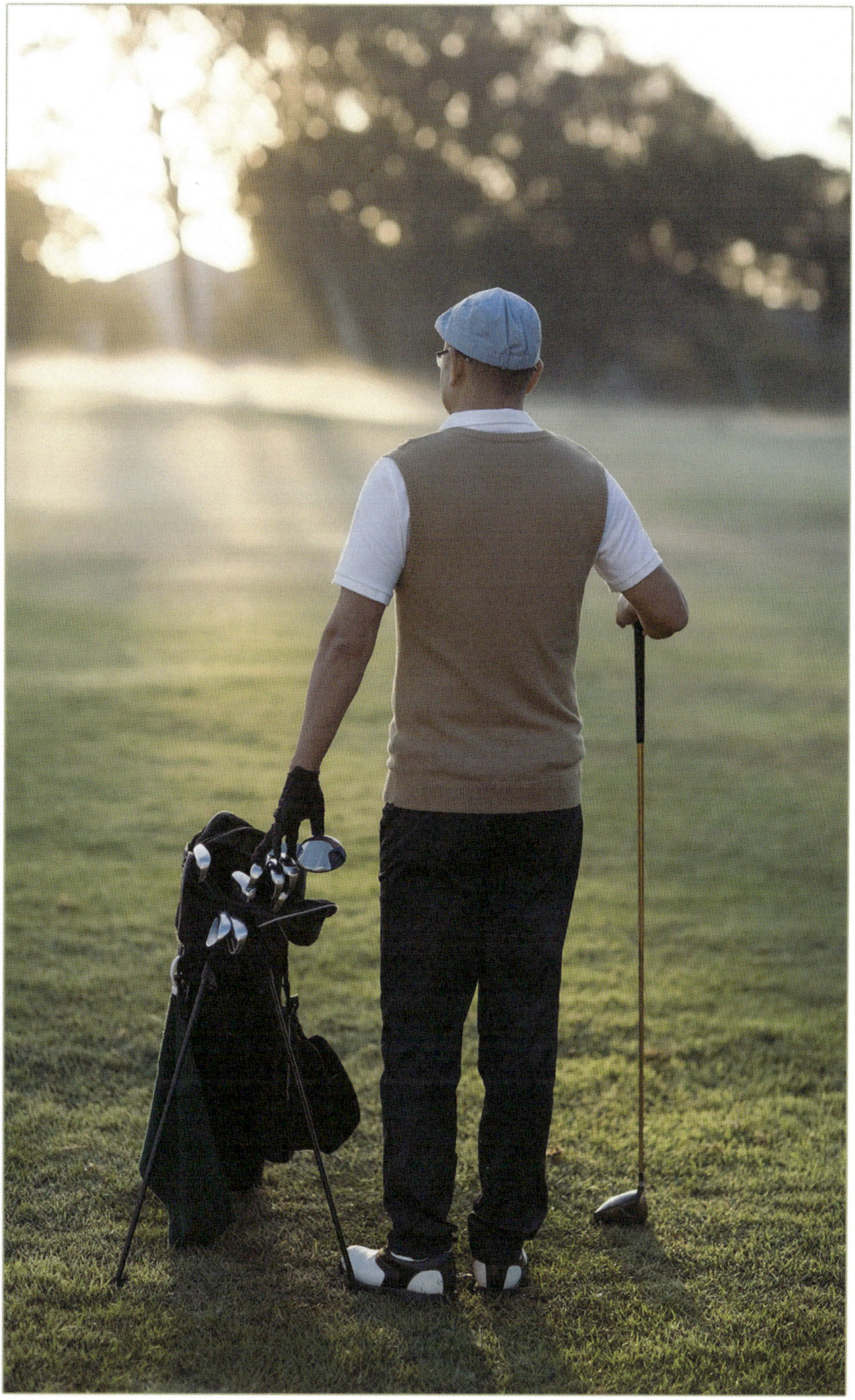

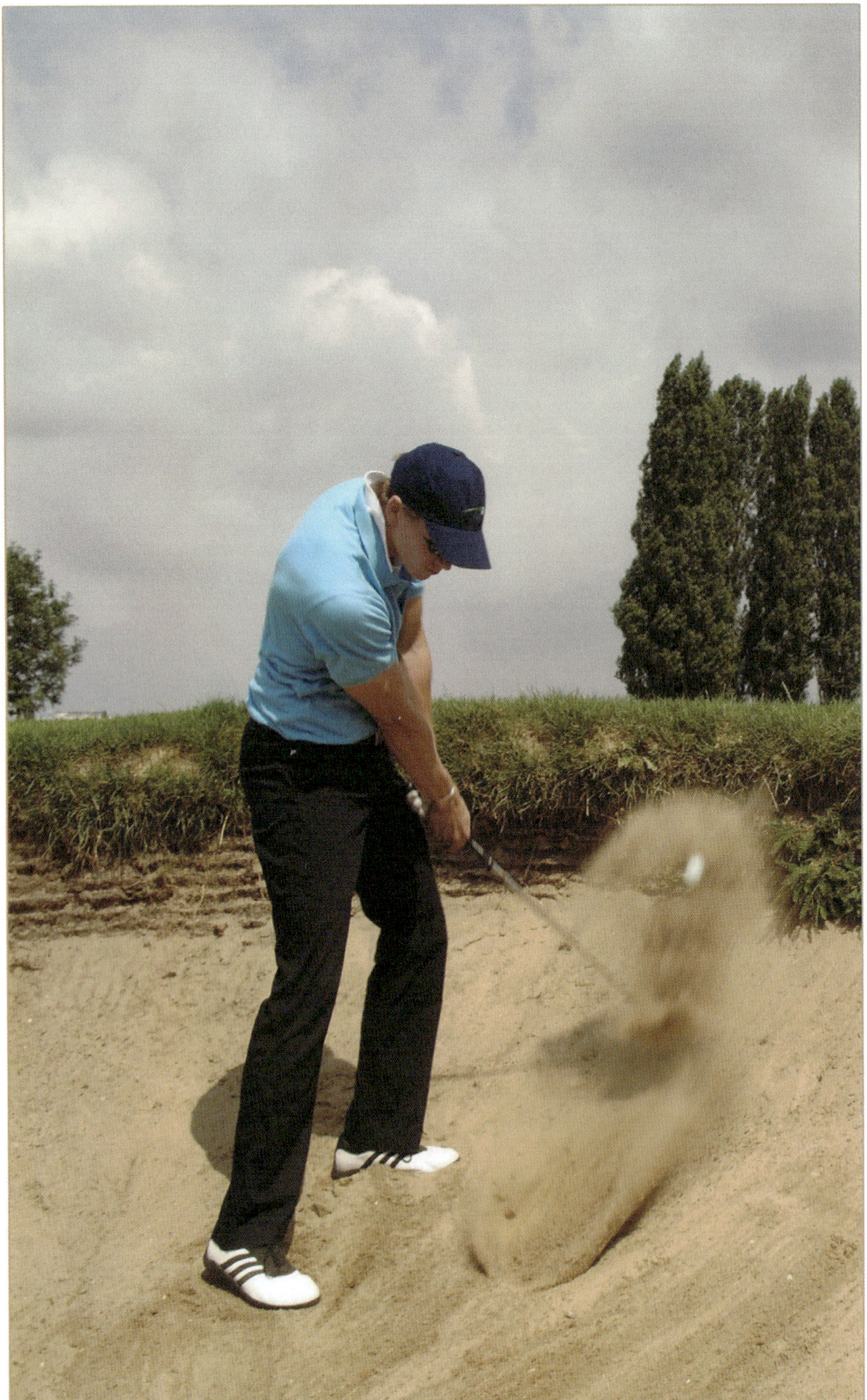

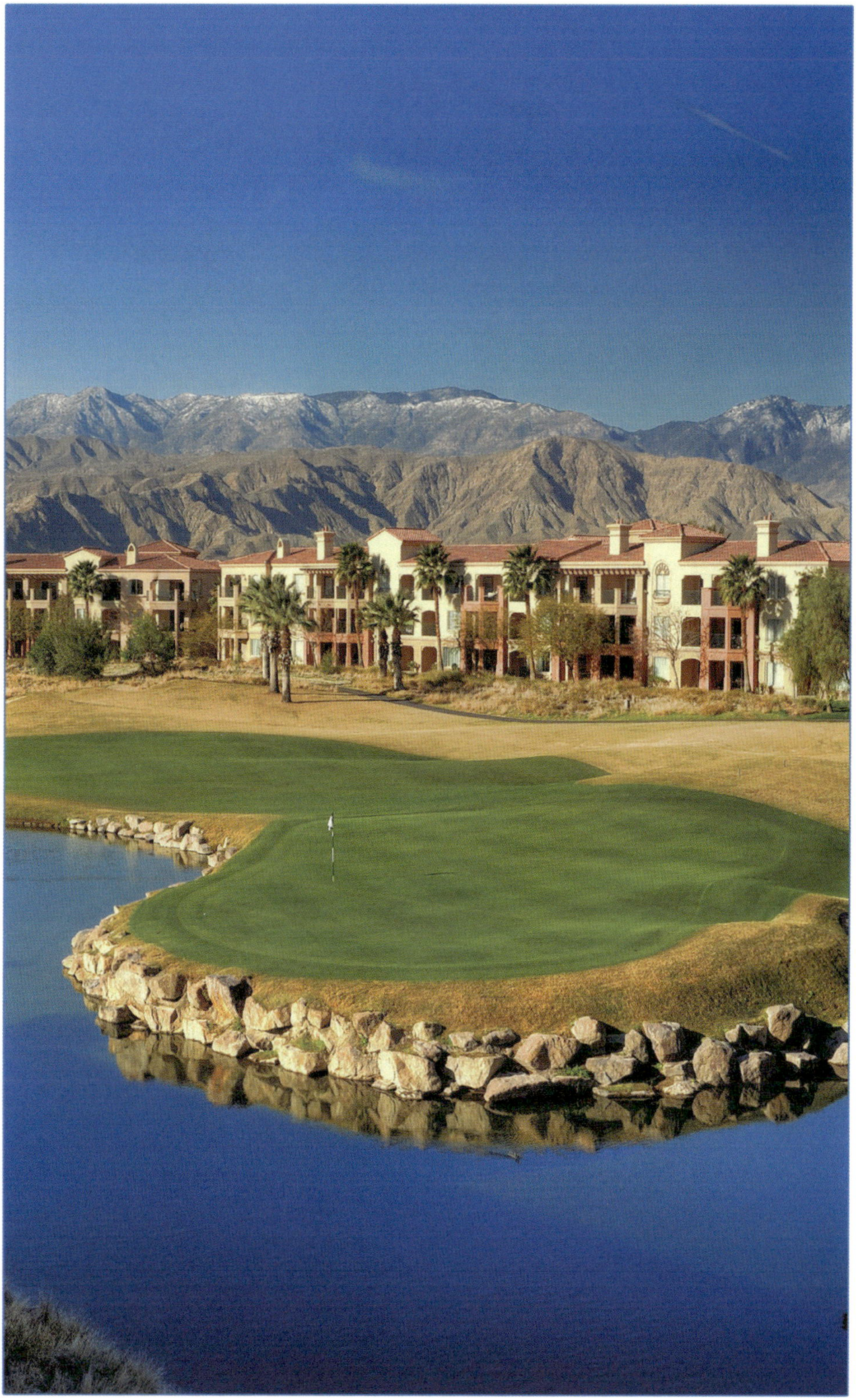

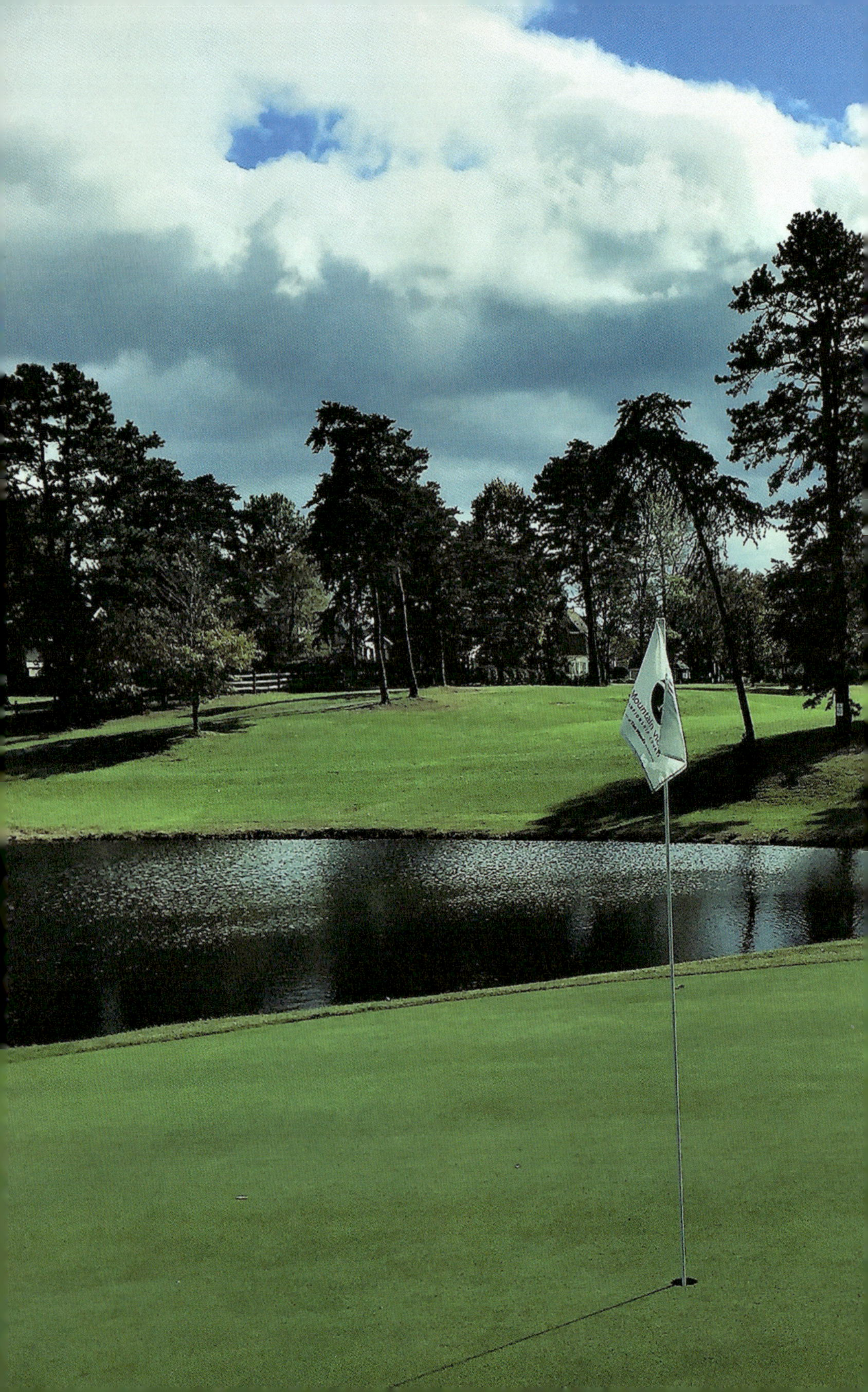

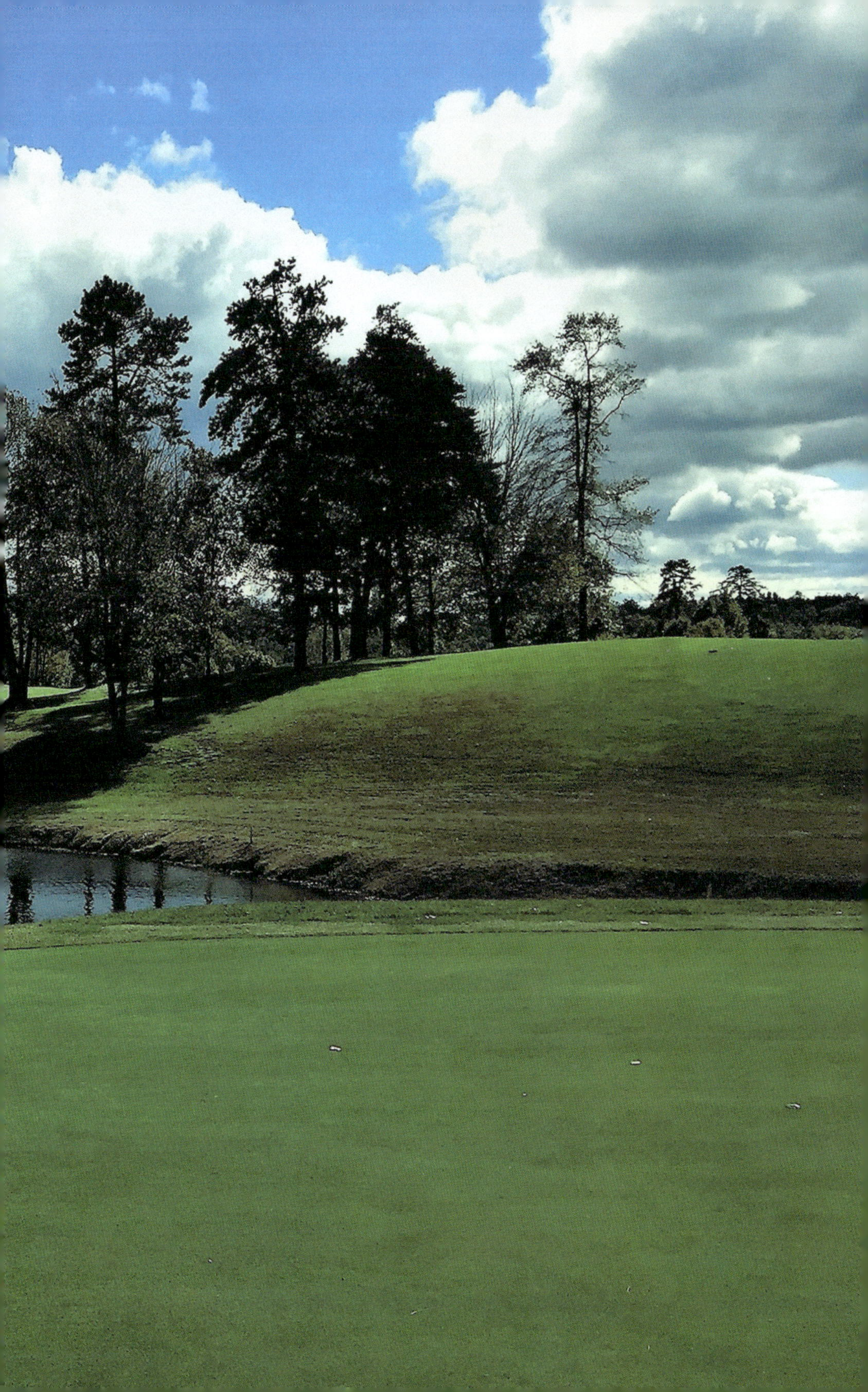

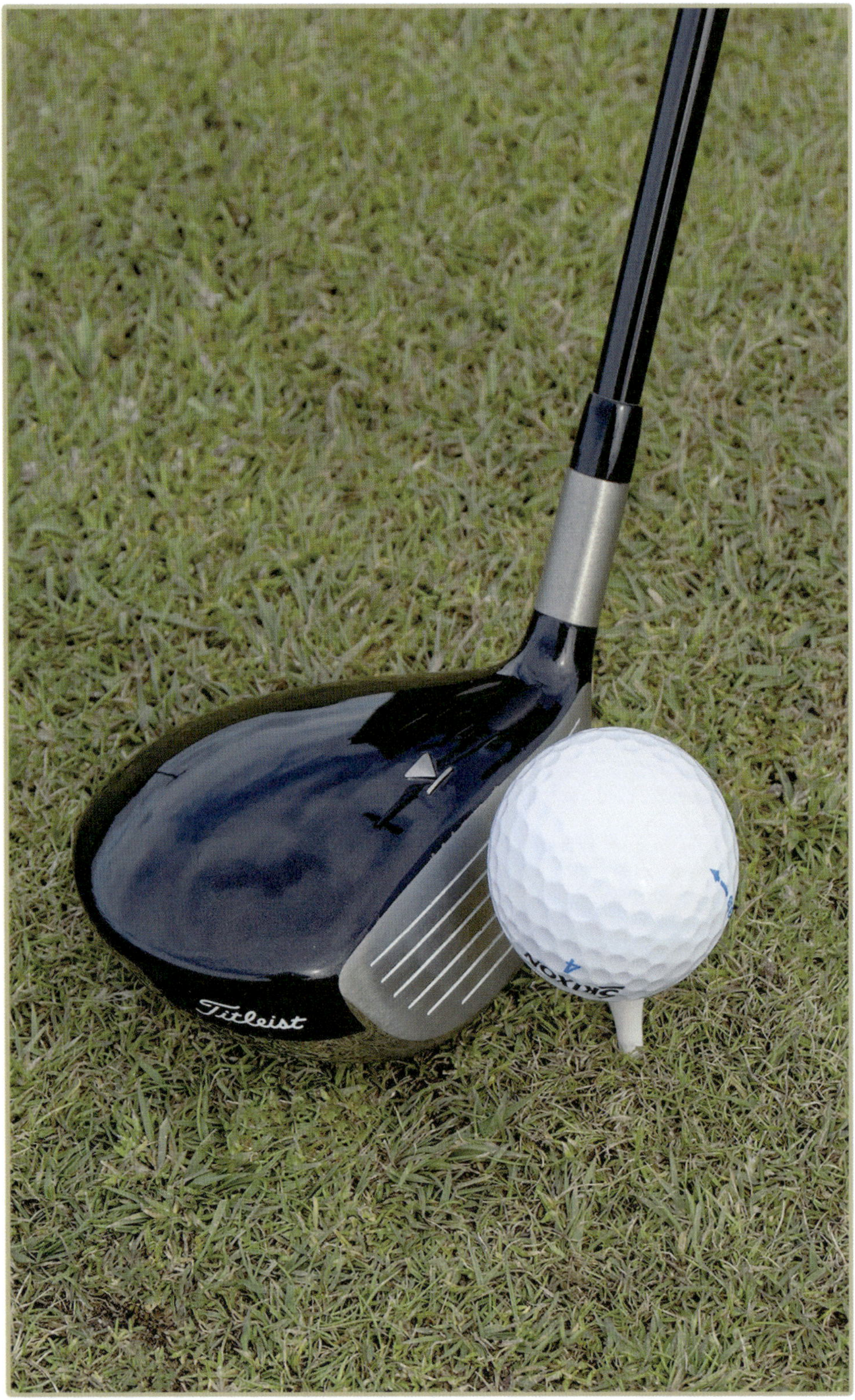
Titleist

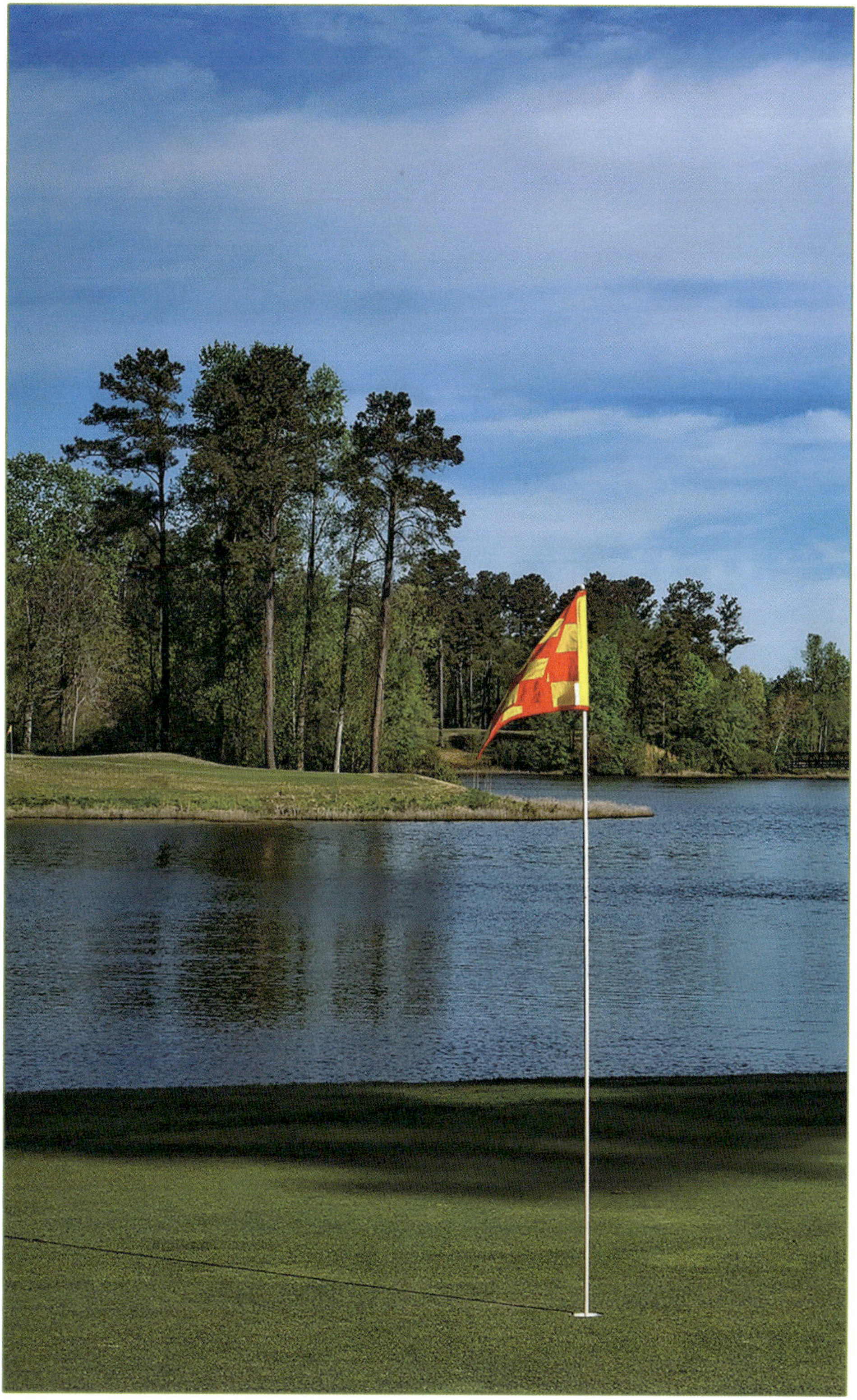

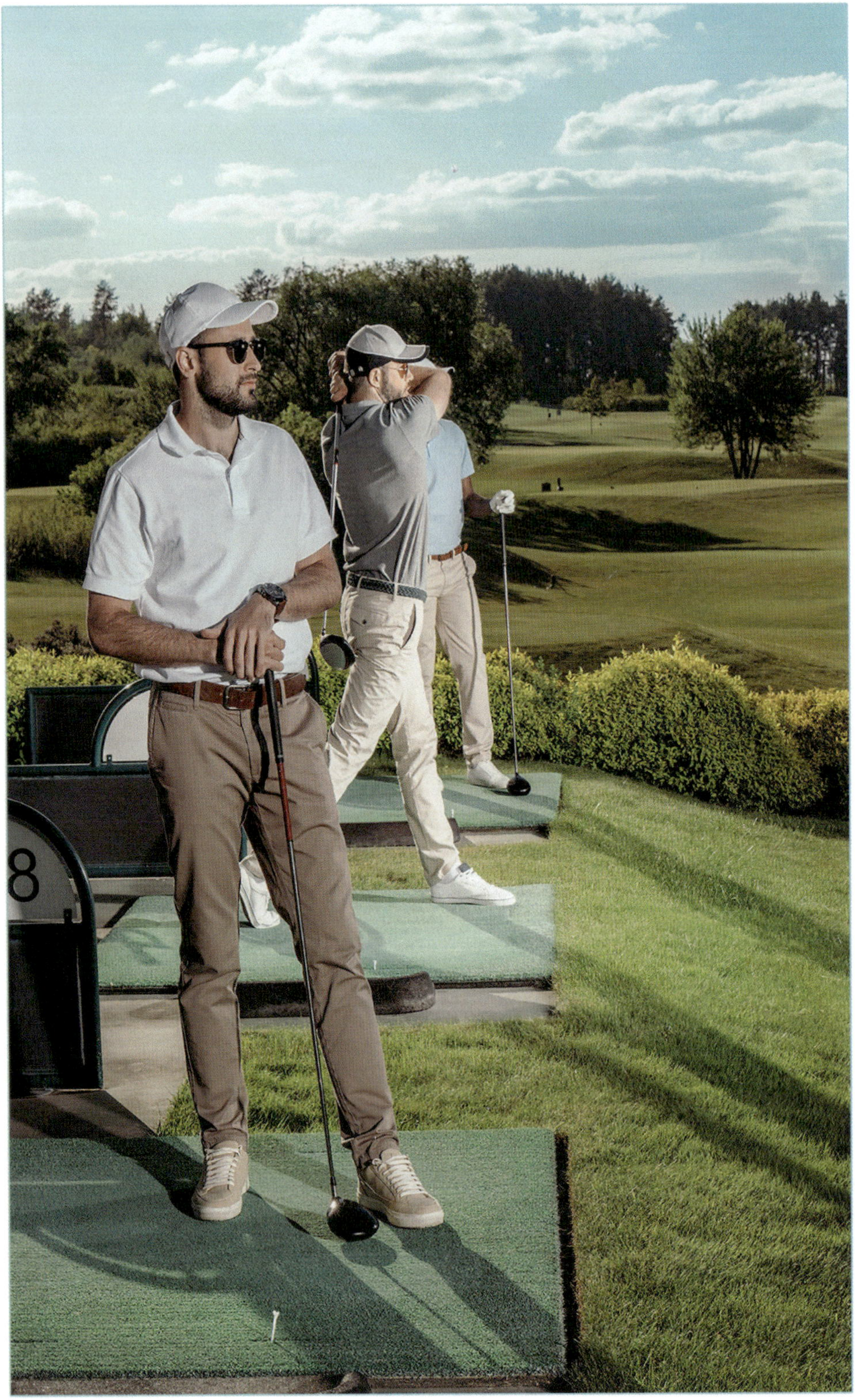
8

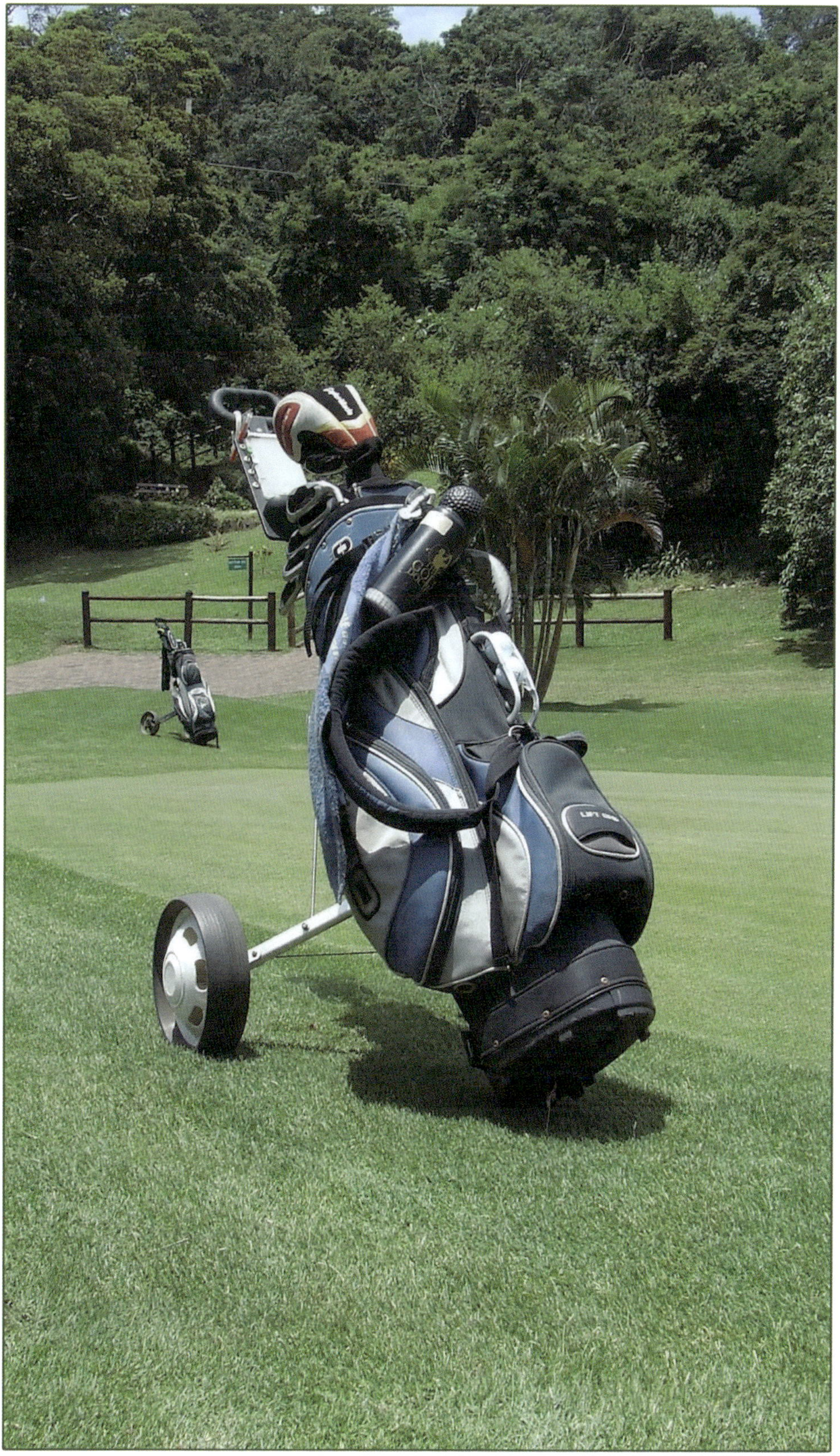

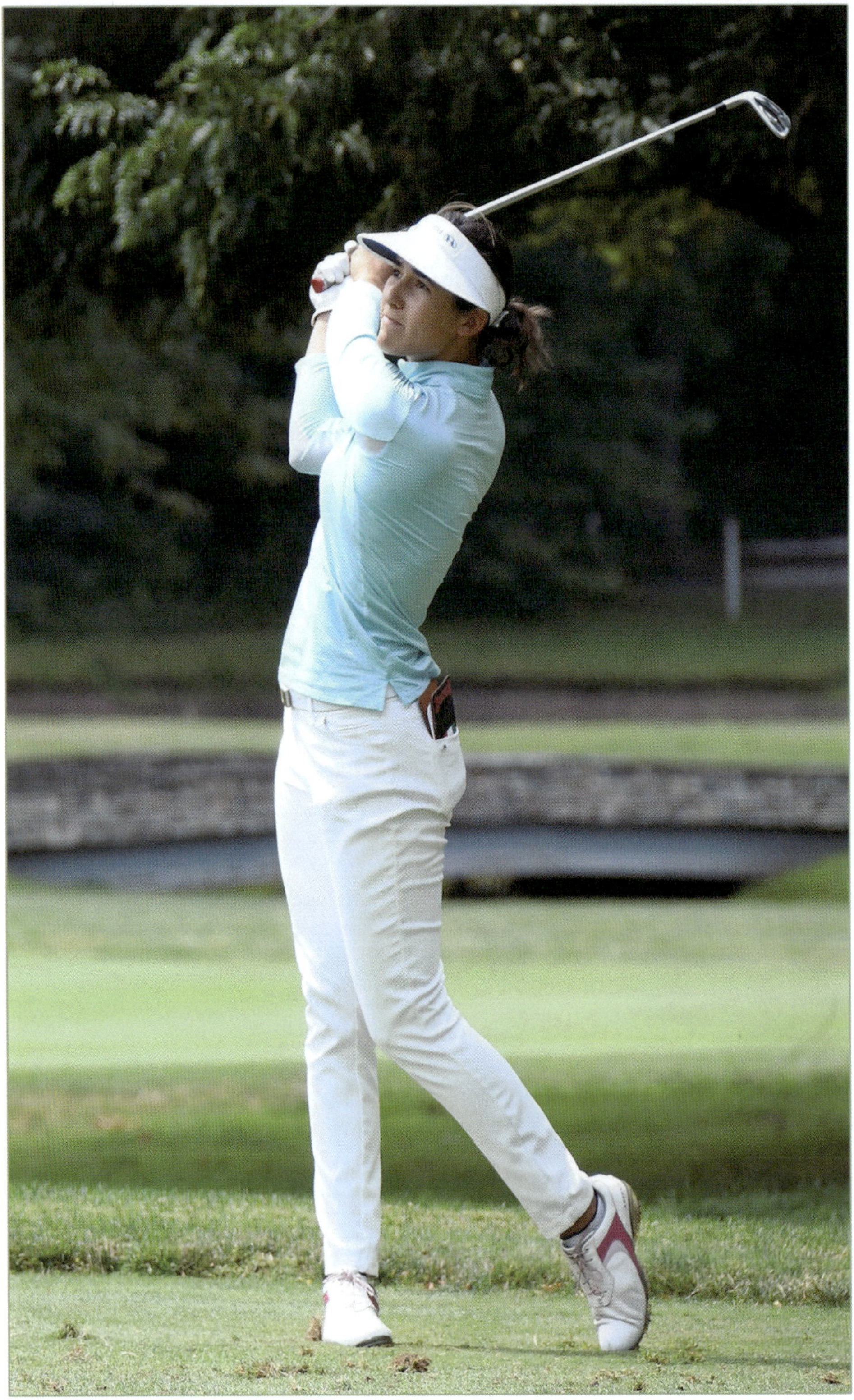

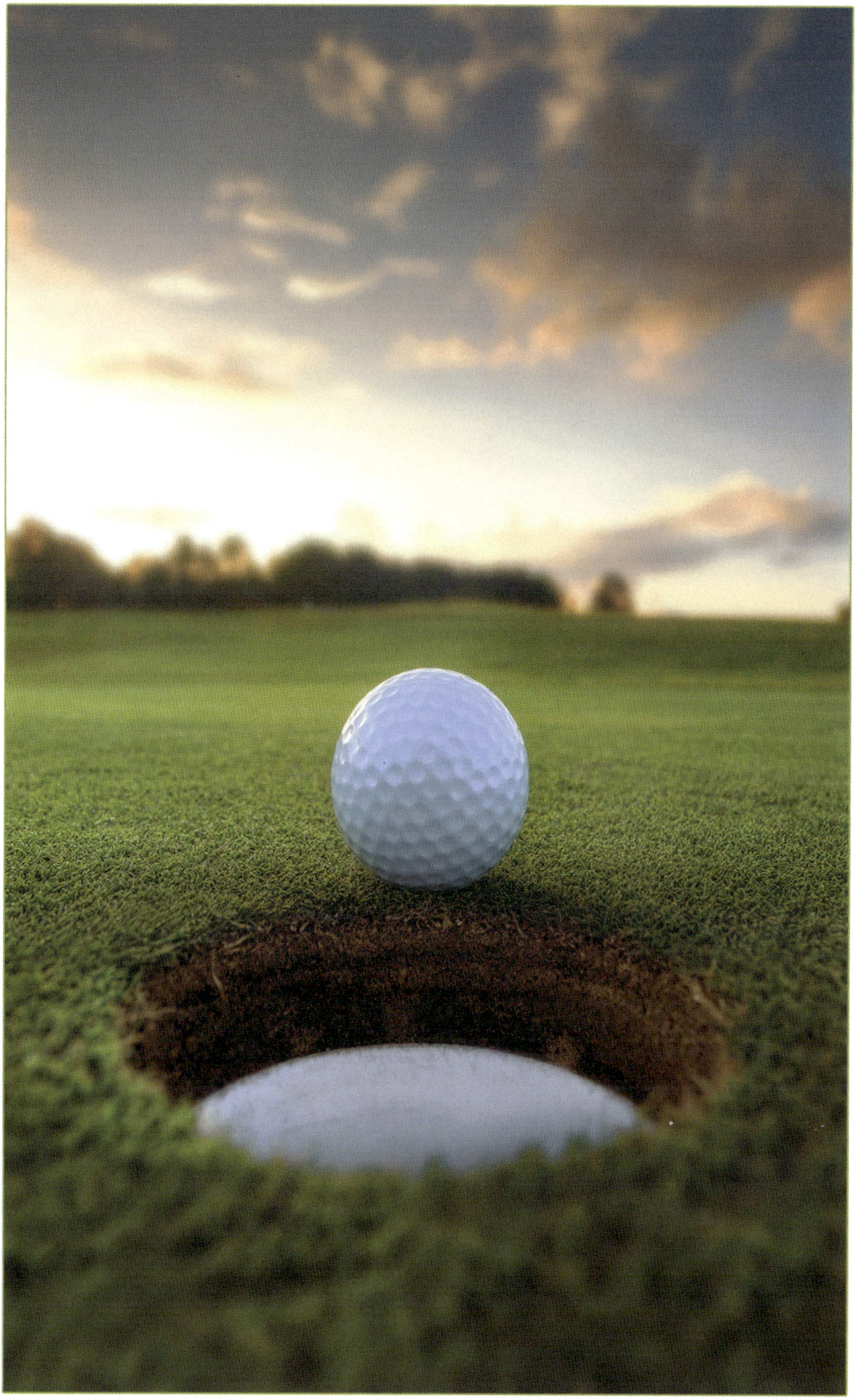

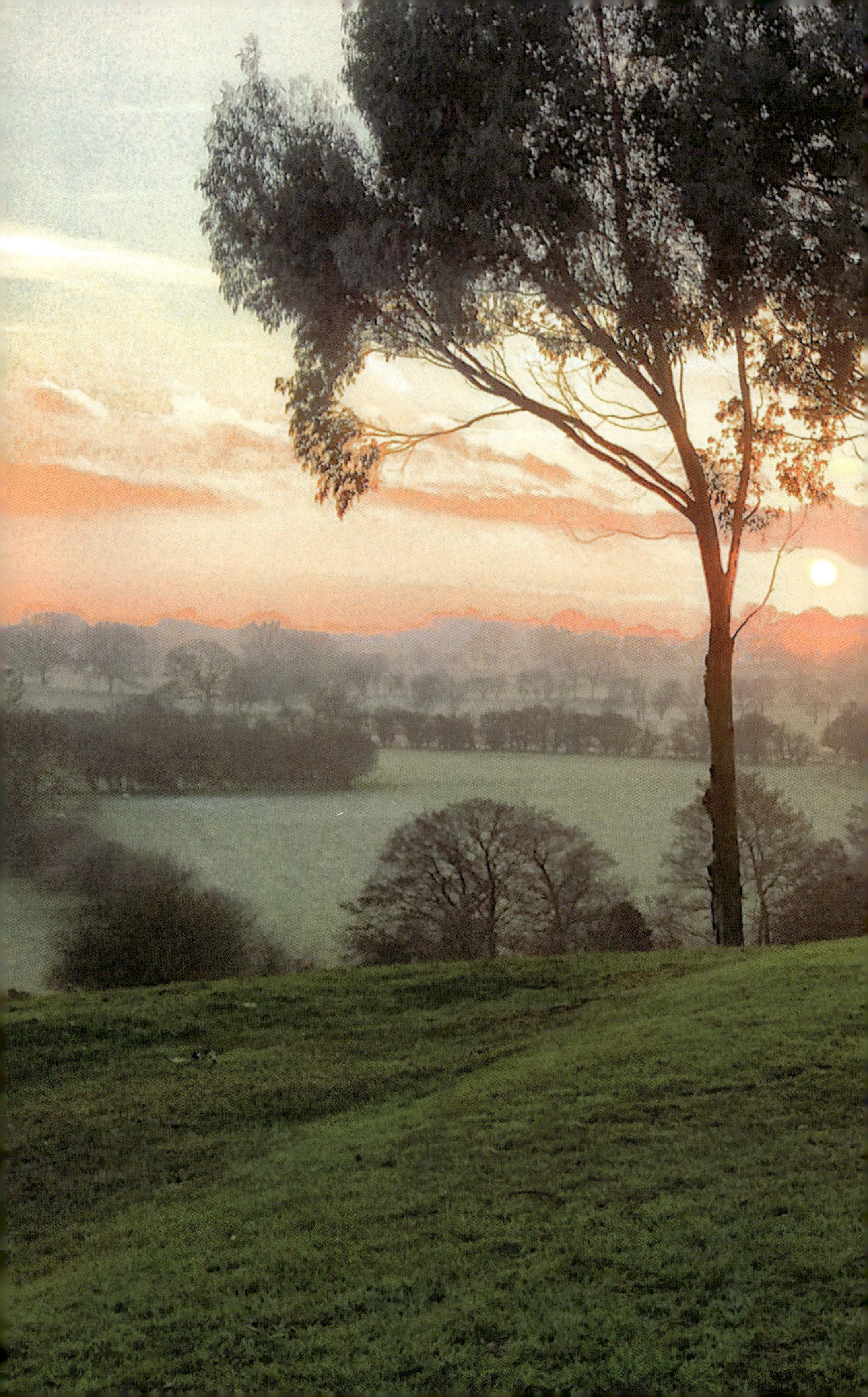

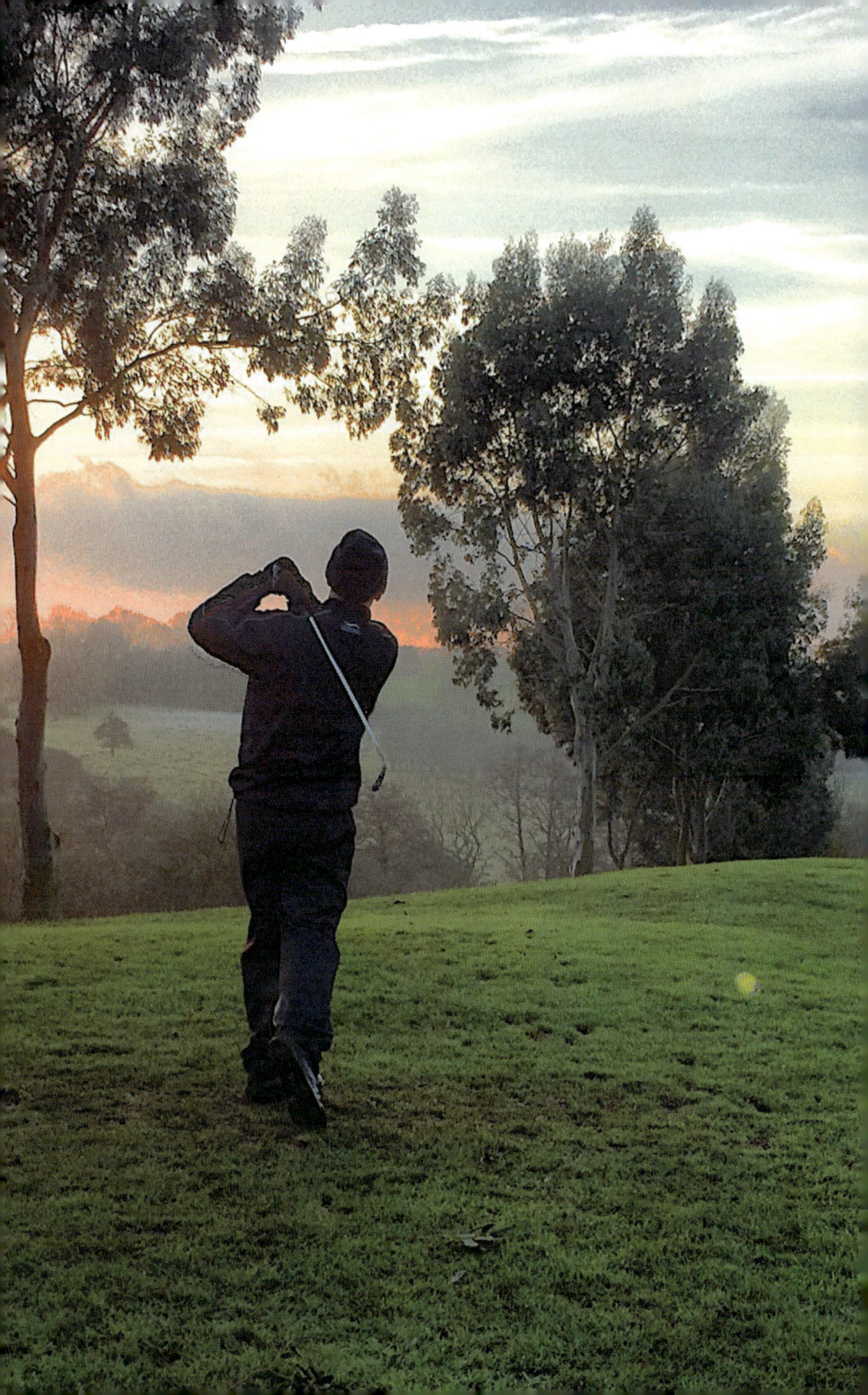

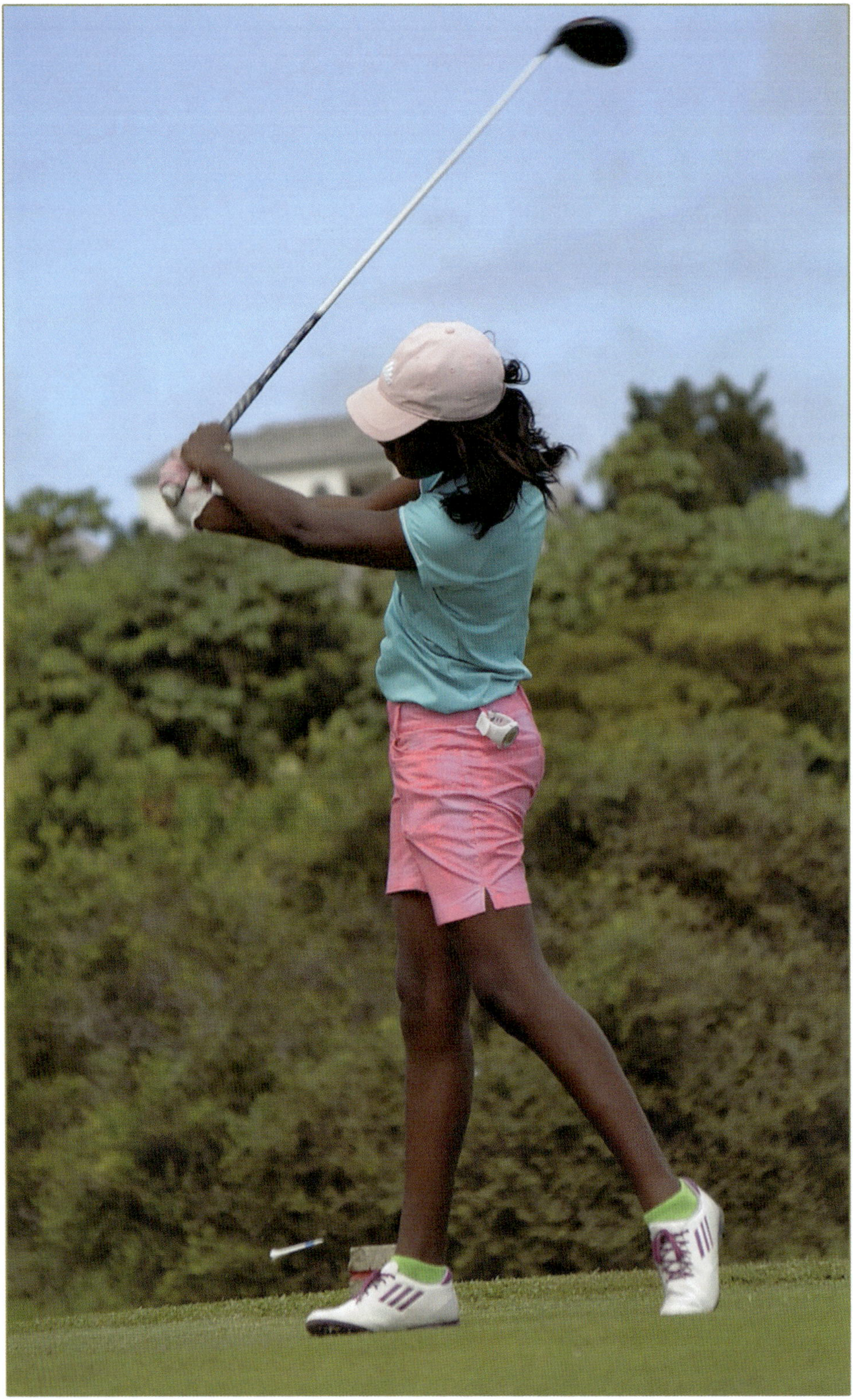

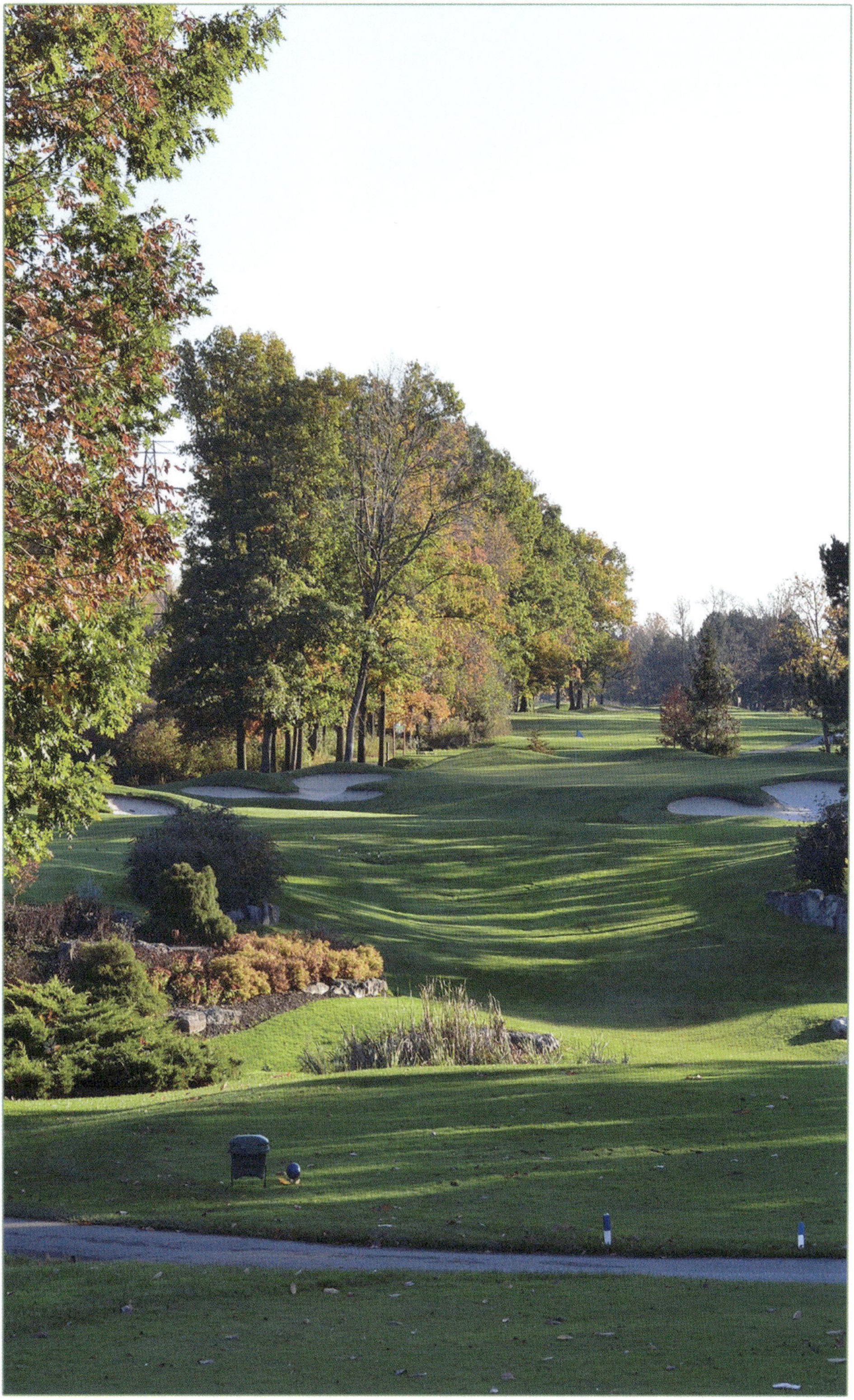

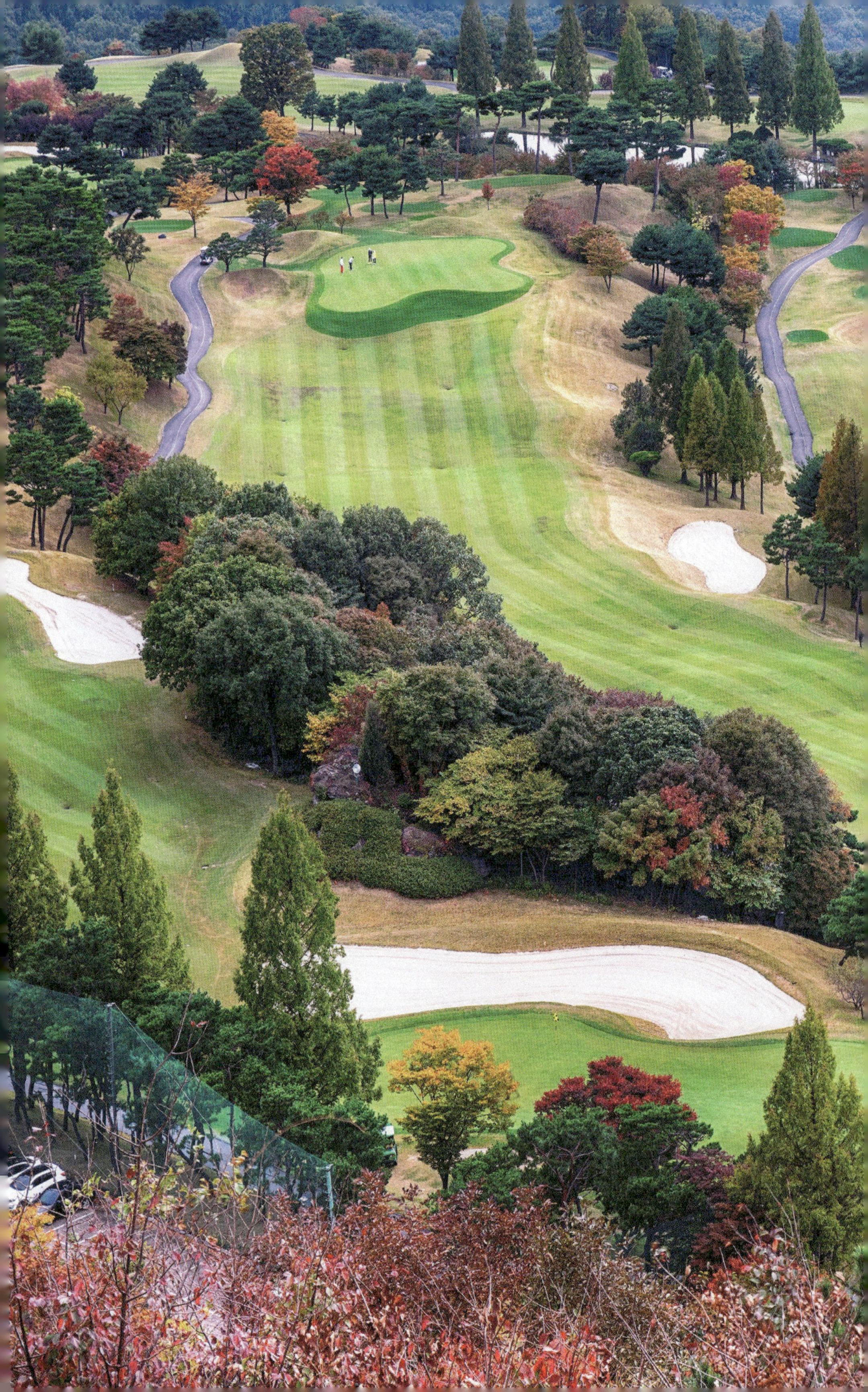

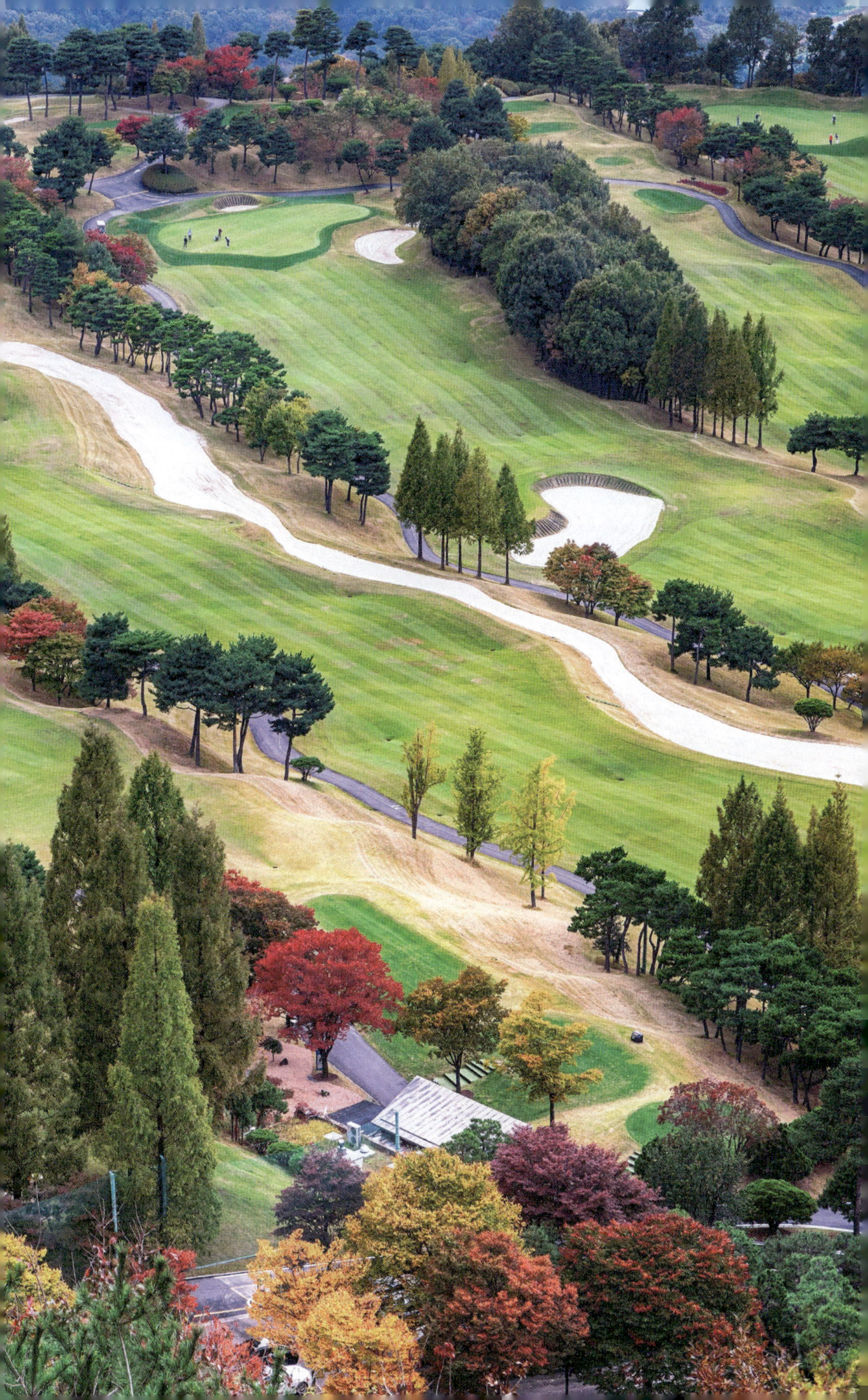

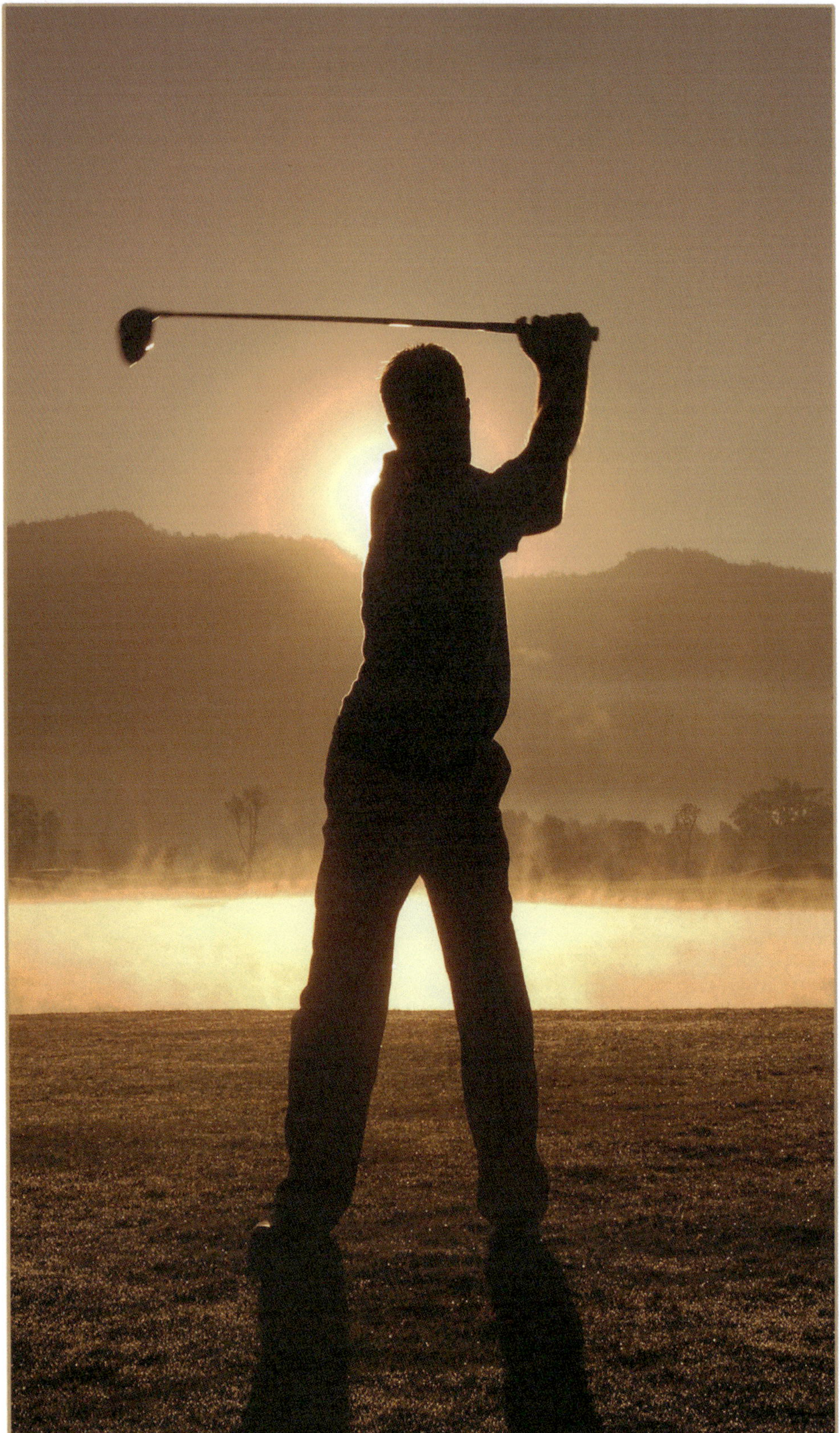

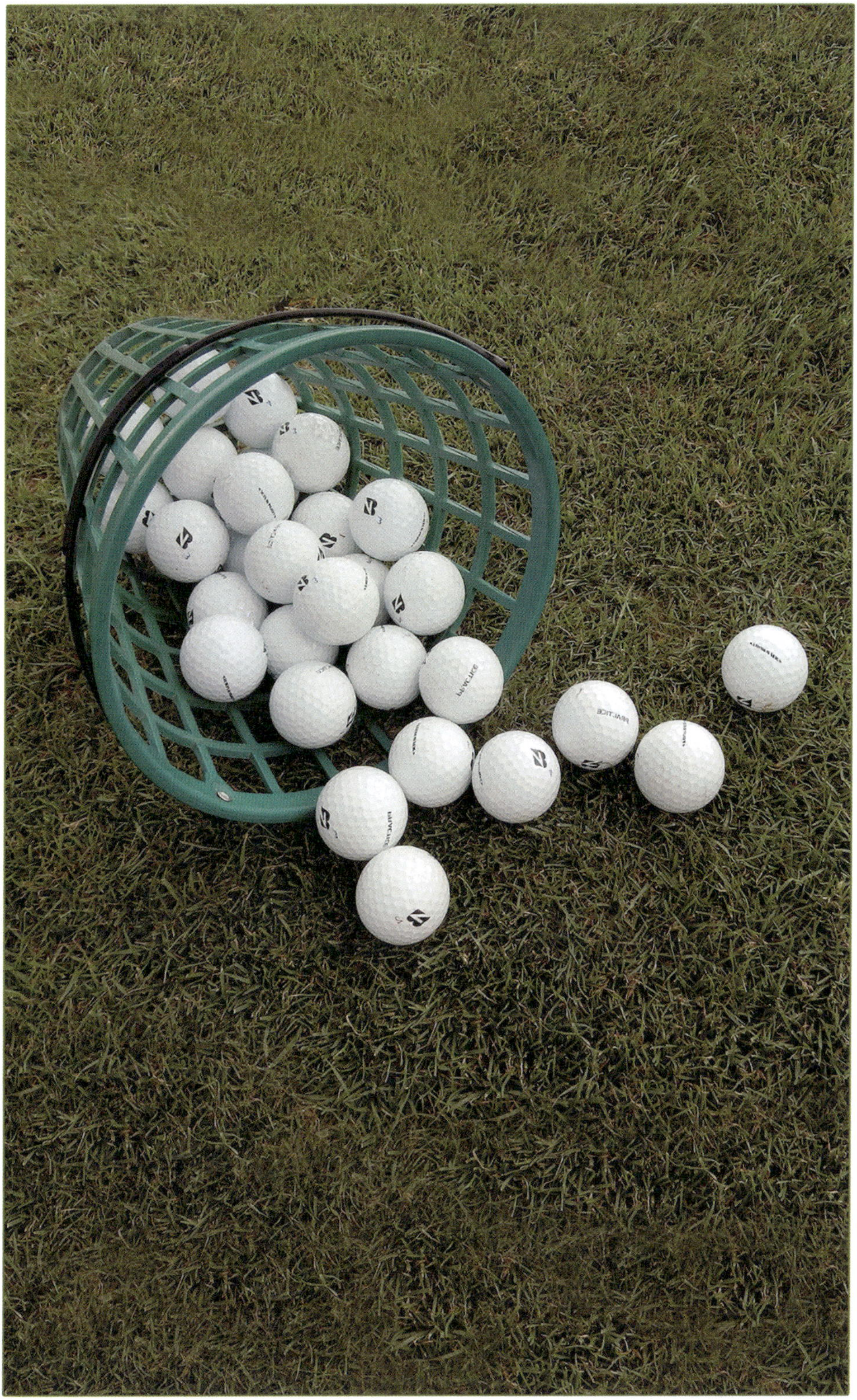

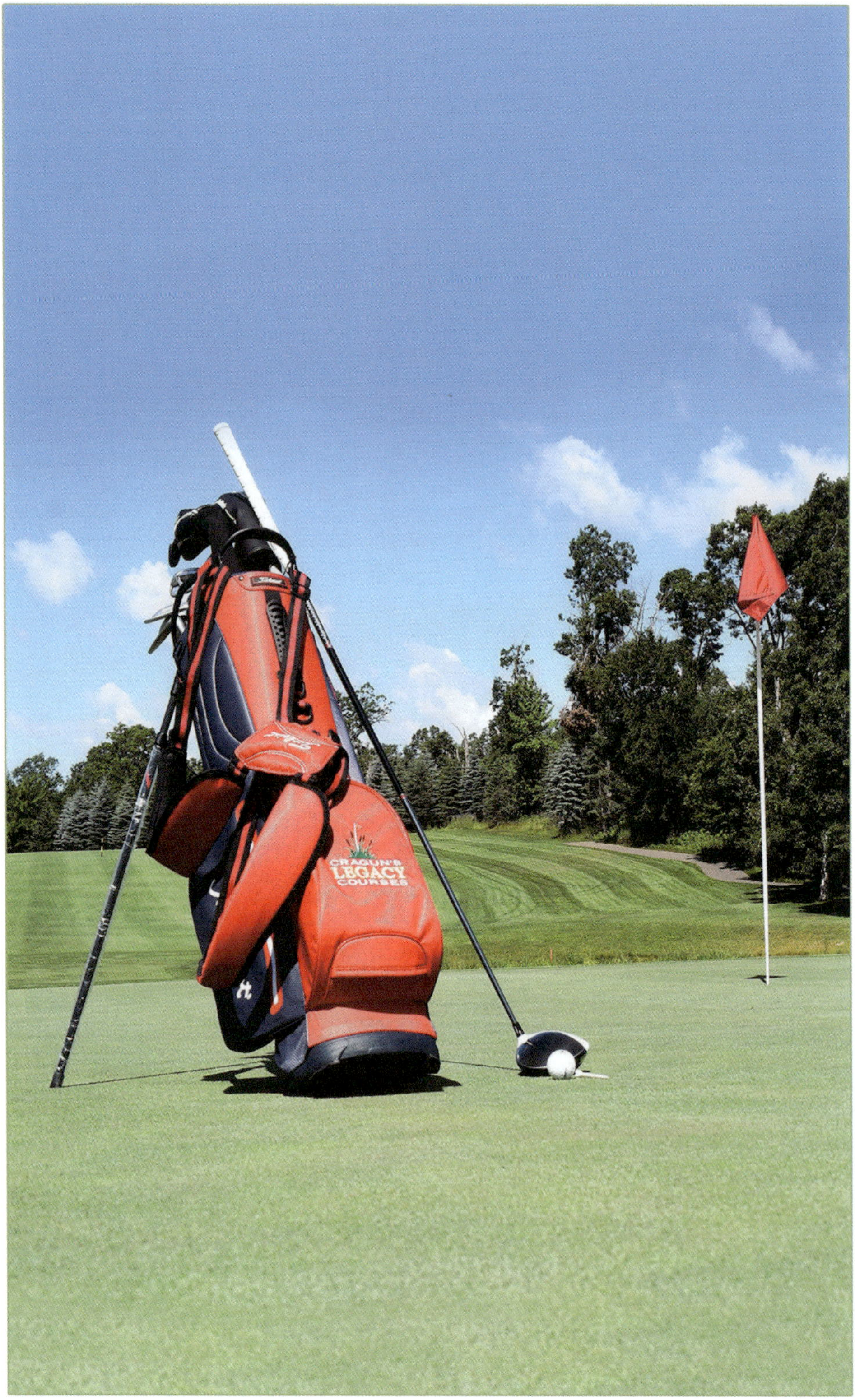
CRAGUN'S
LEGACY
COURSES

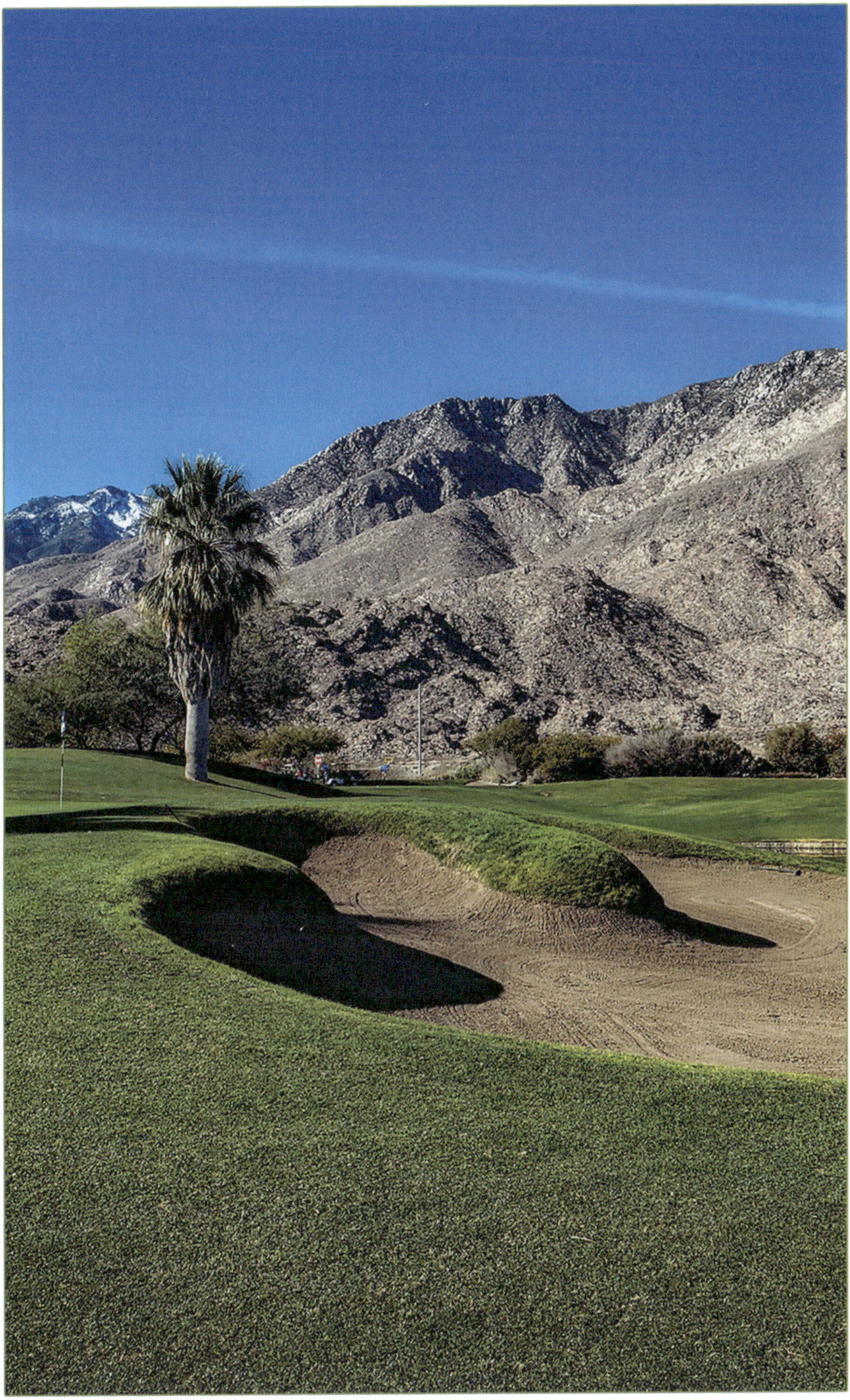

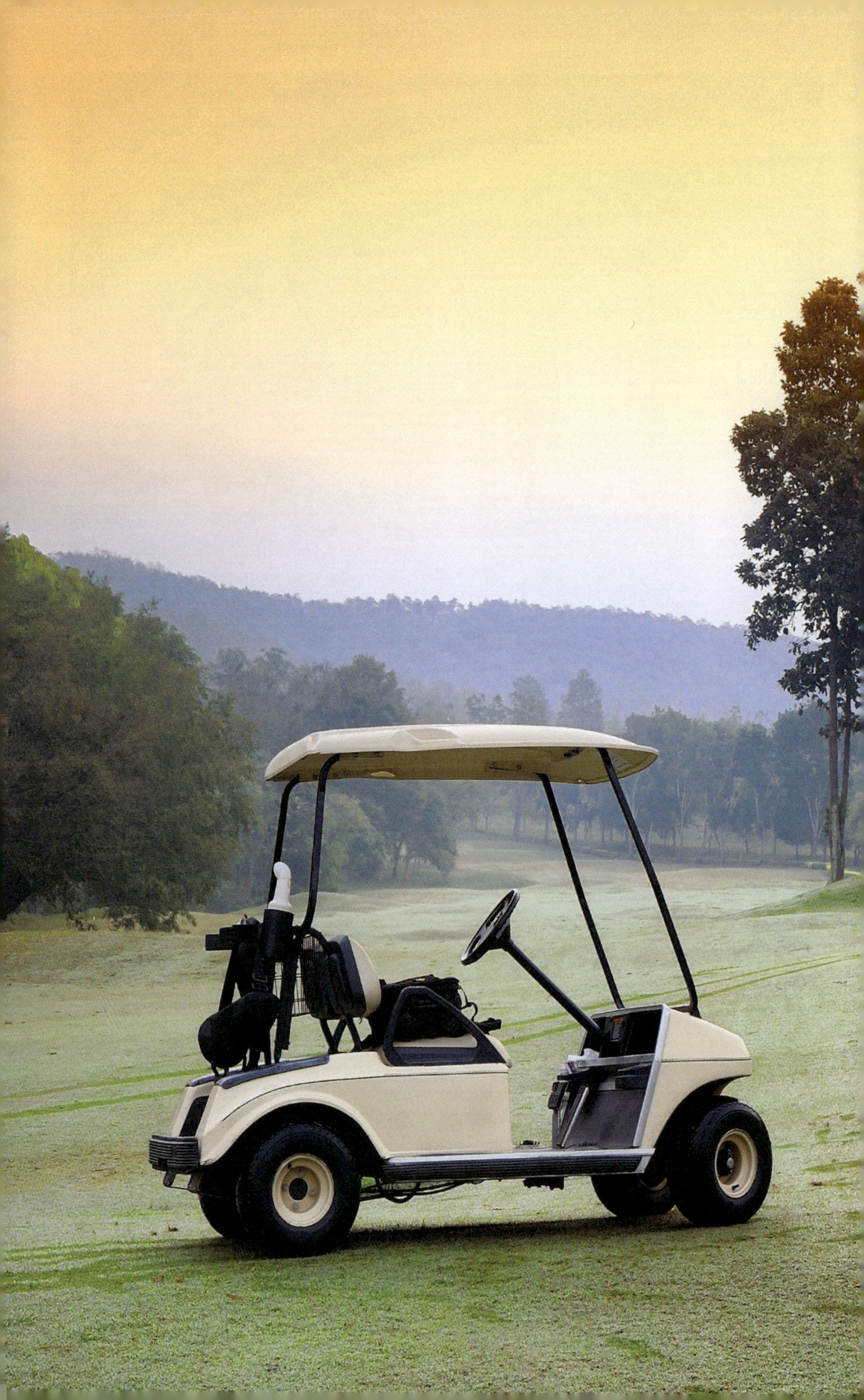

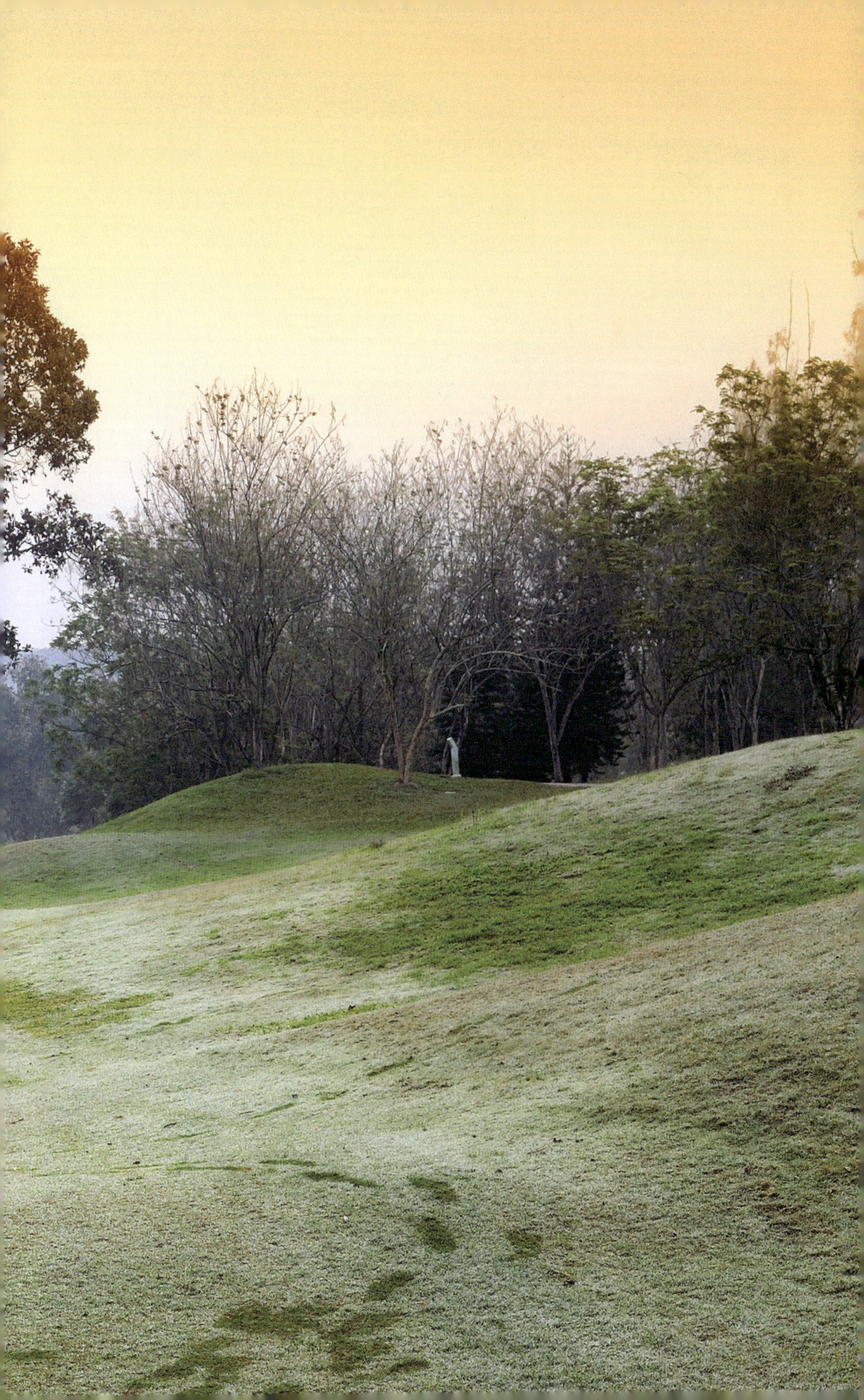

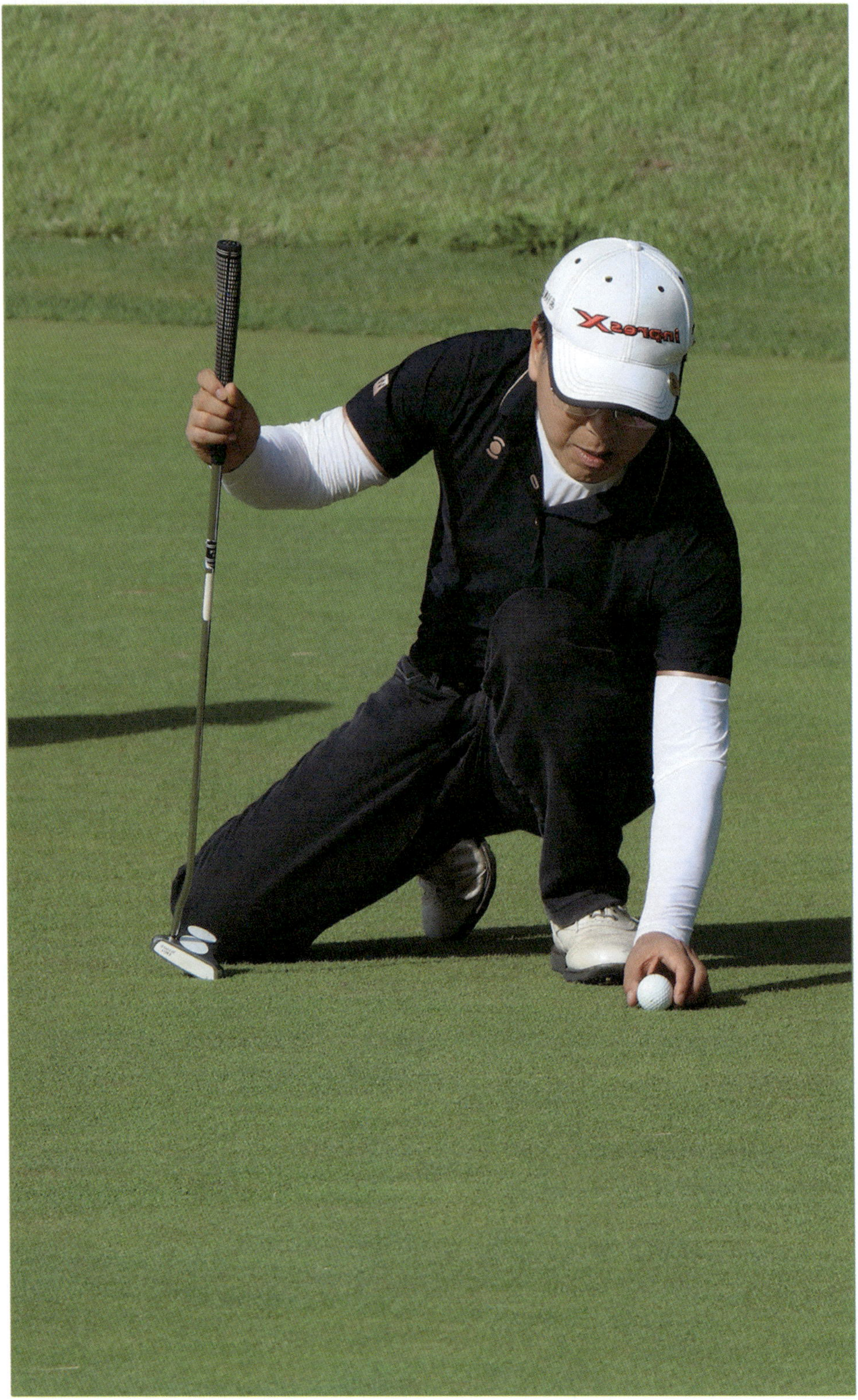
inpresX

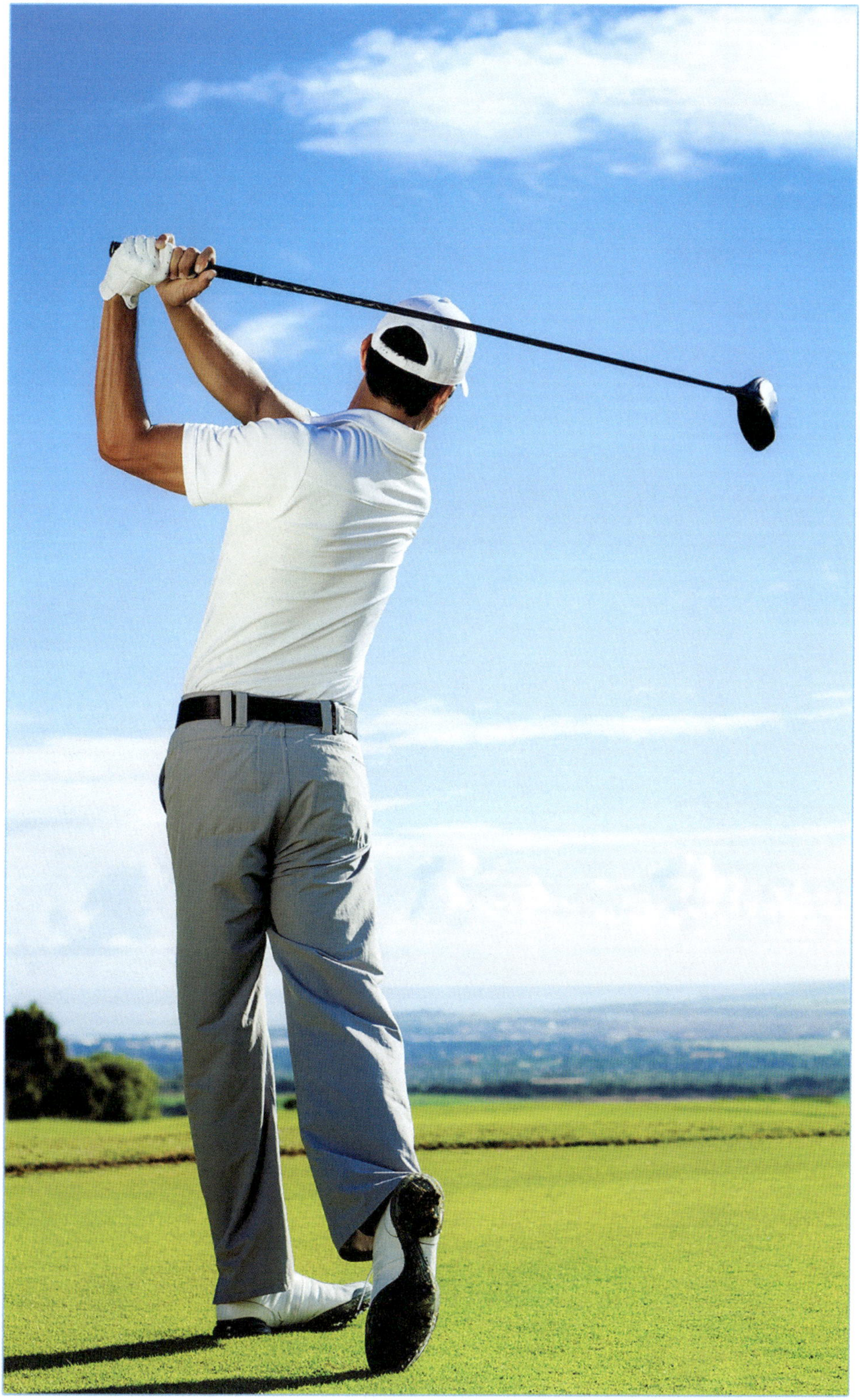

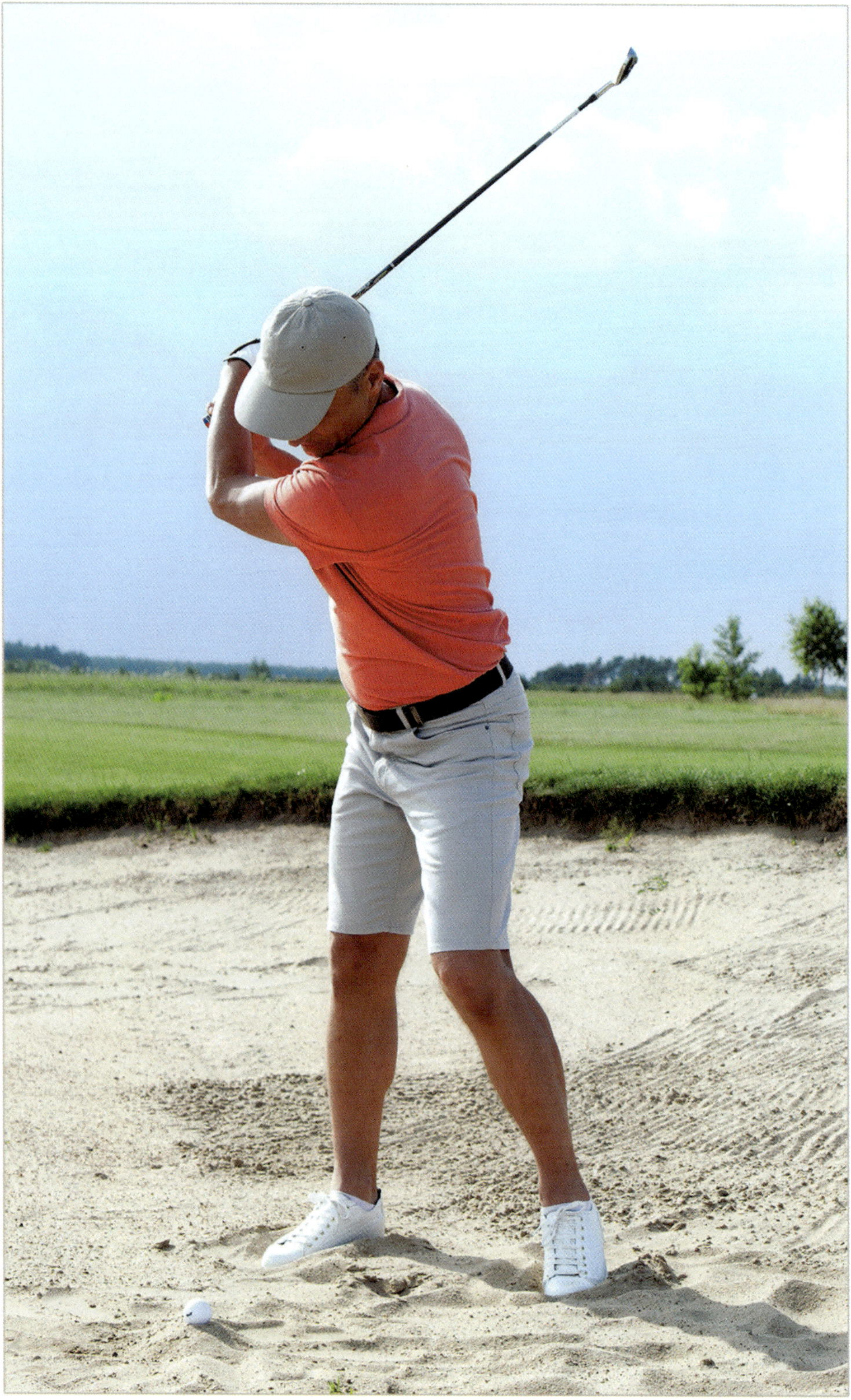

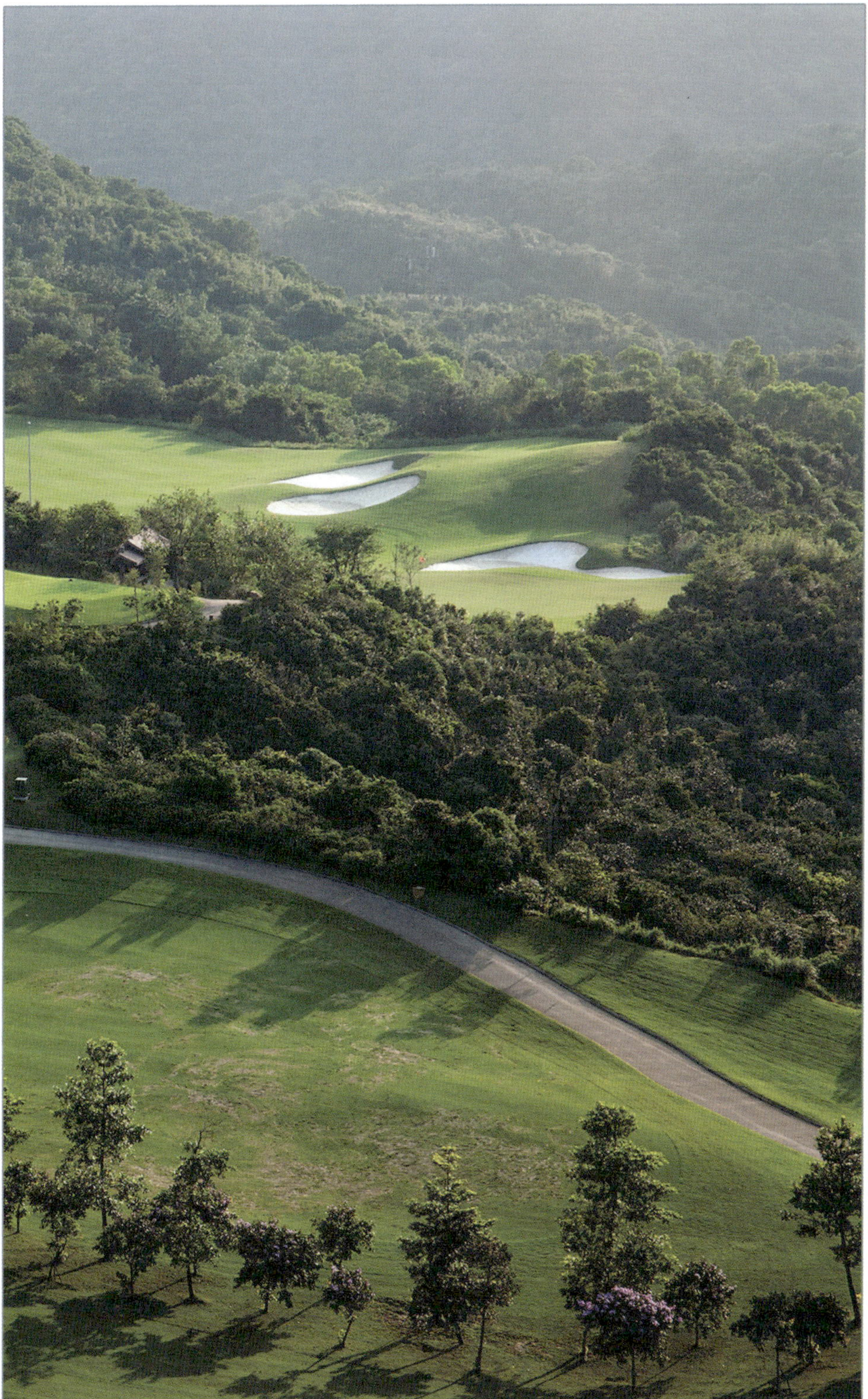

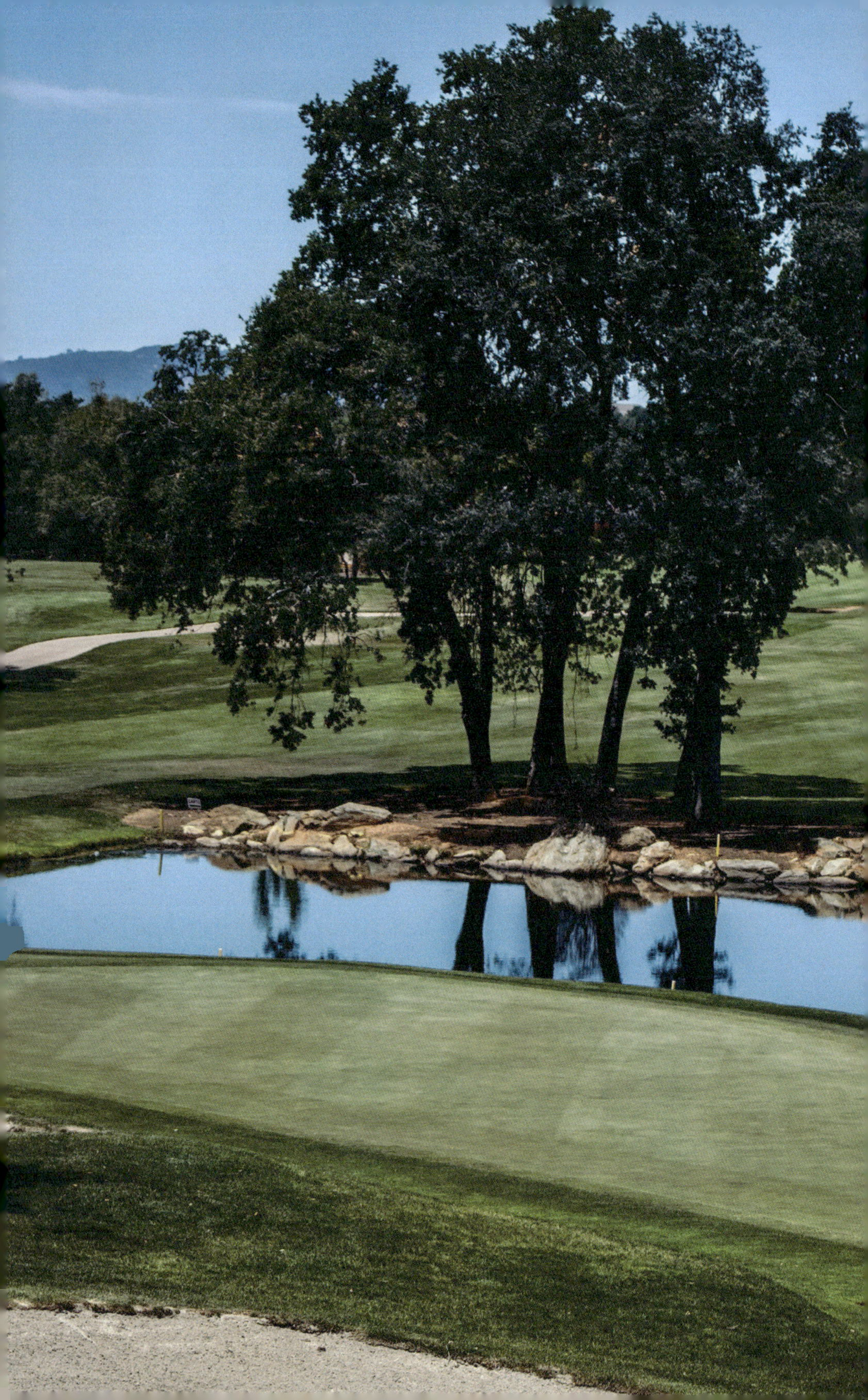

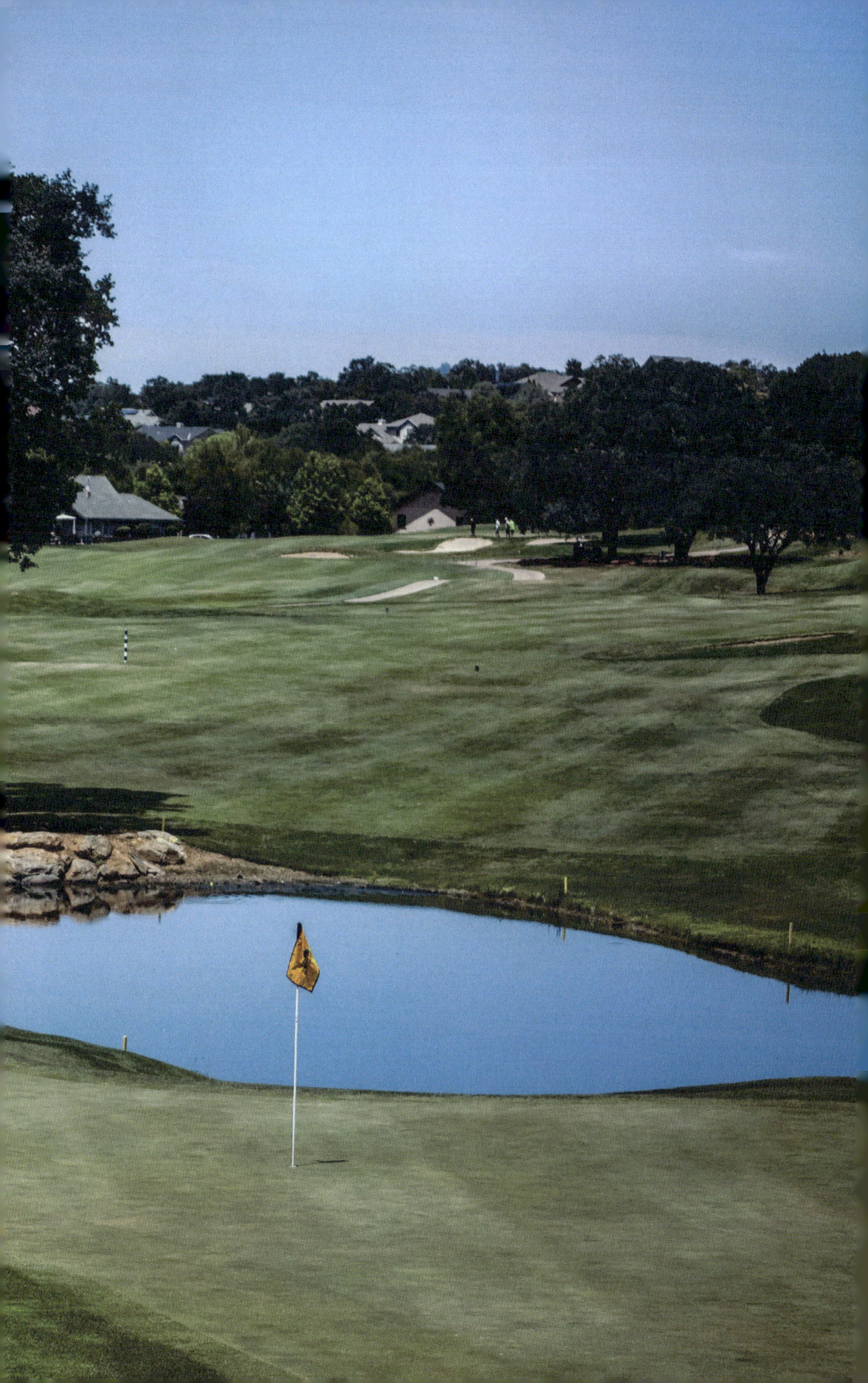

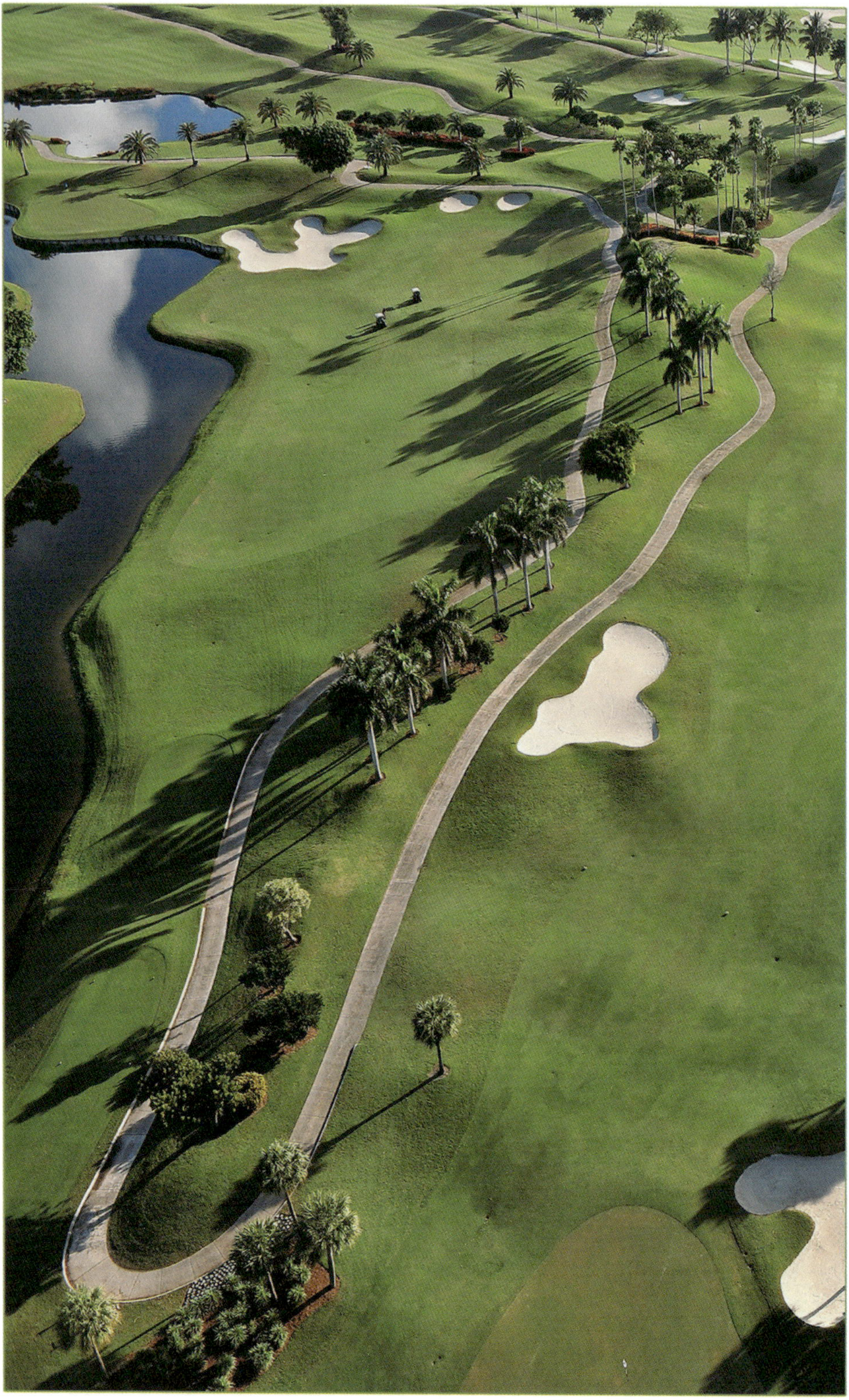

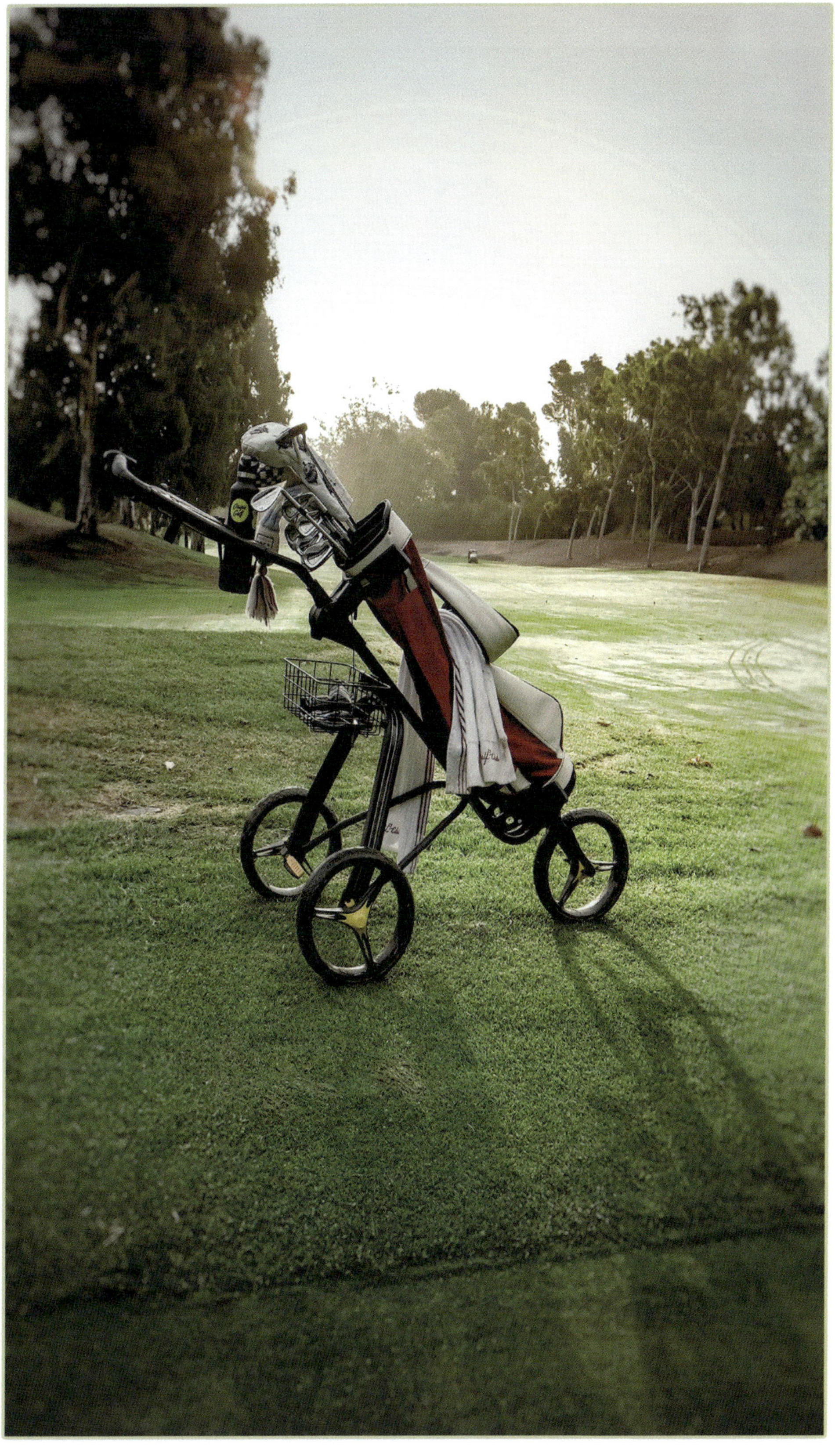

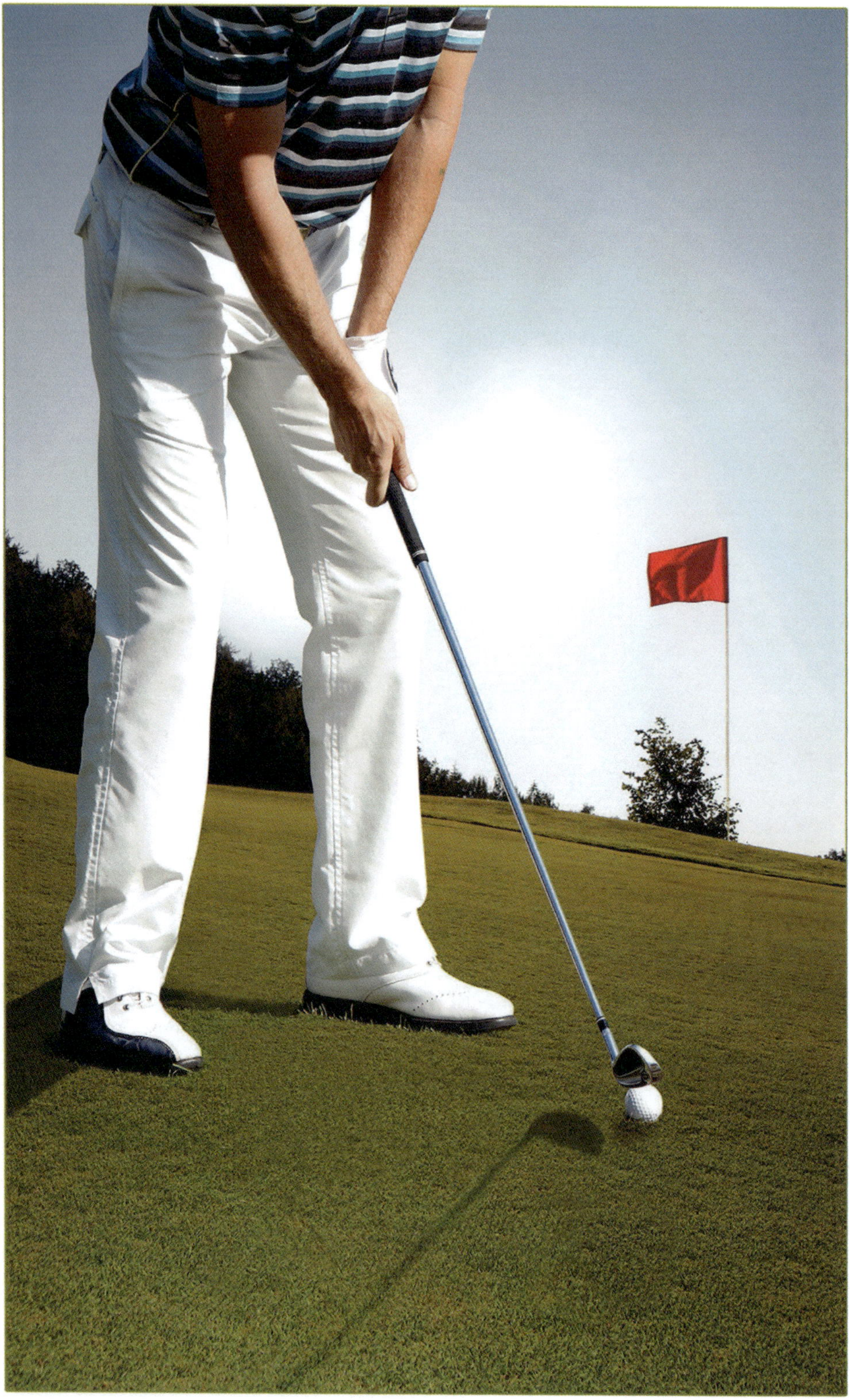

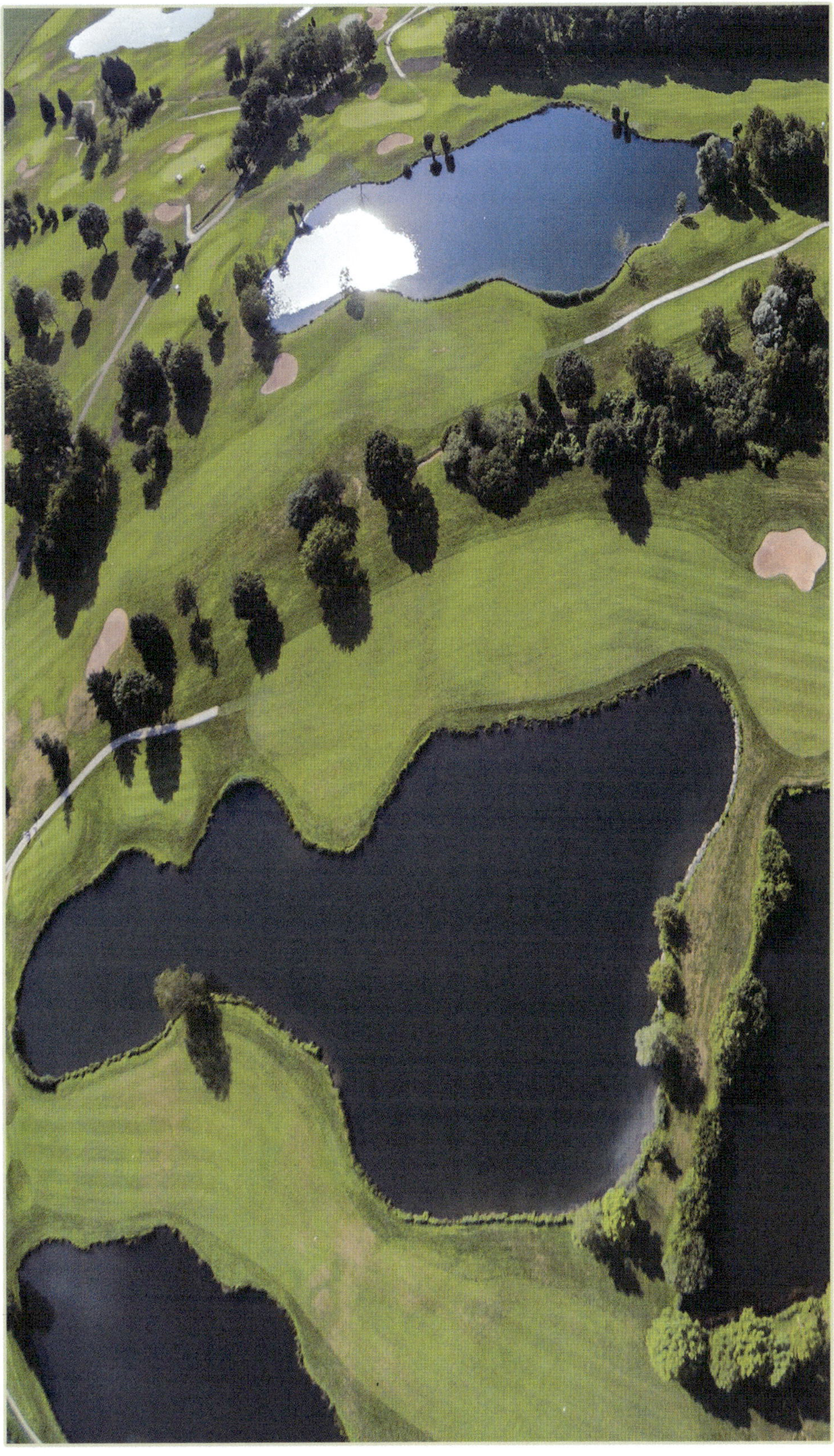

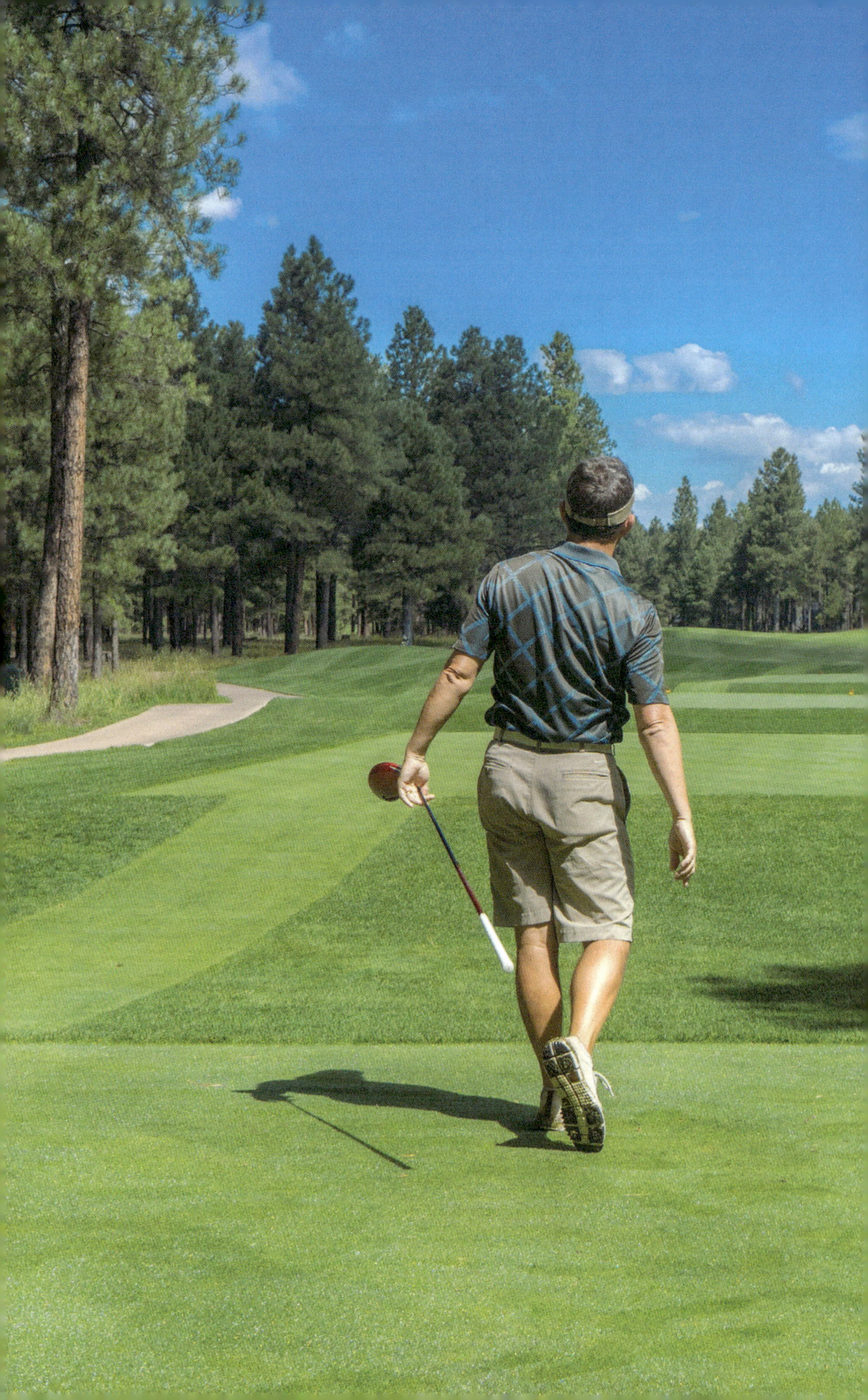

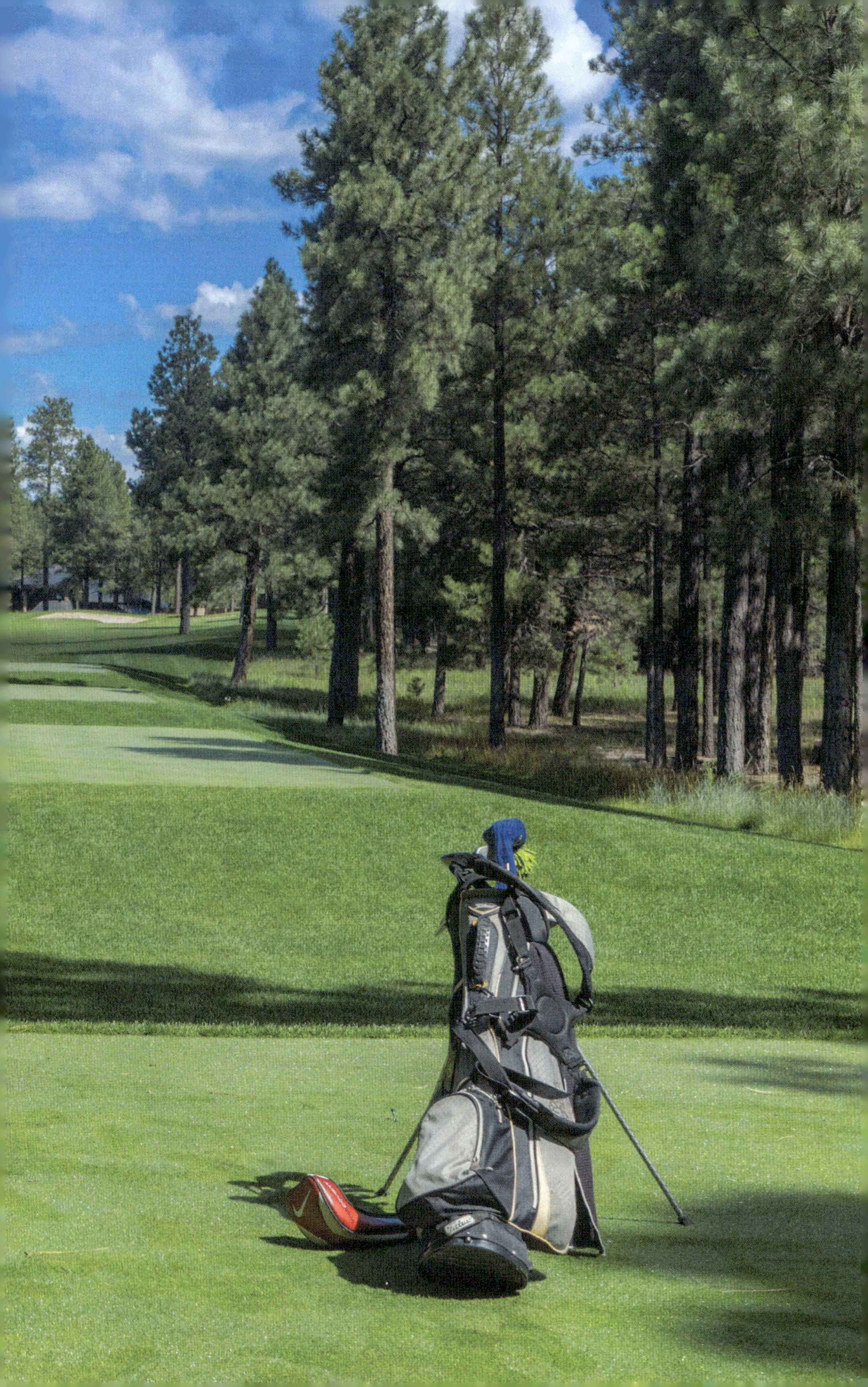

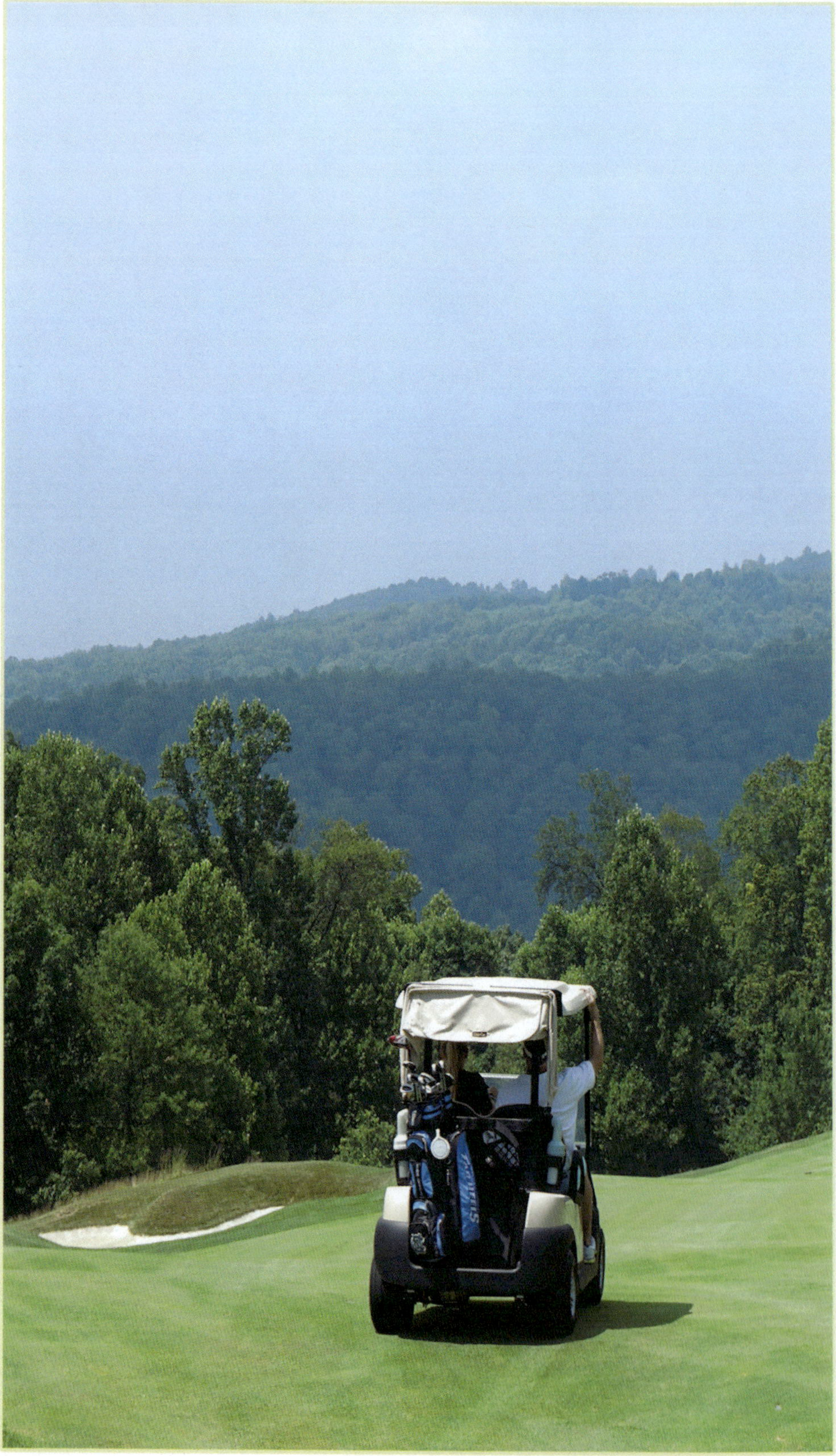

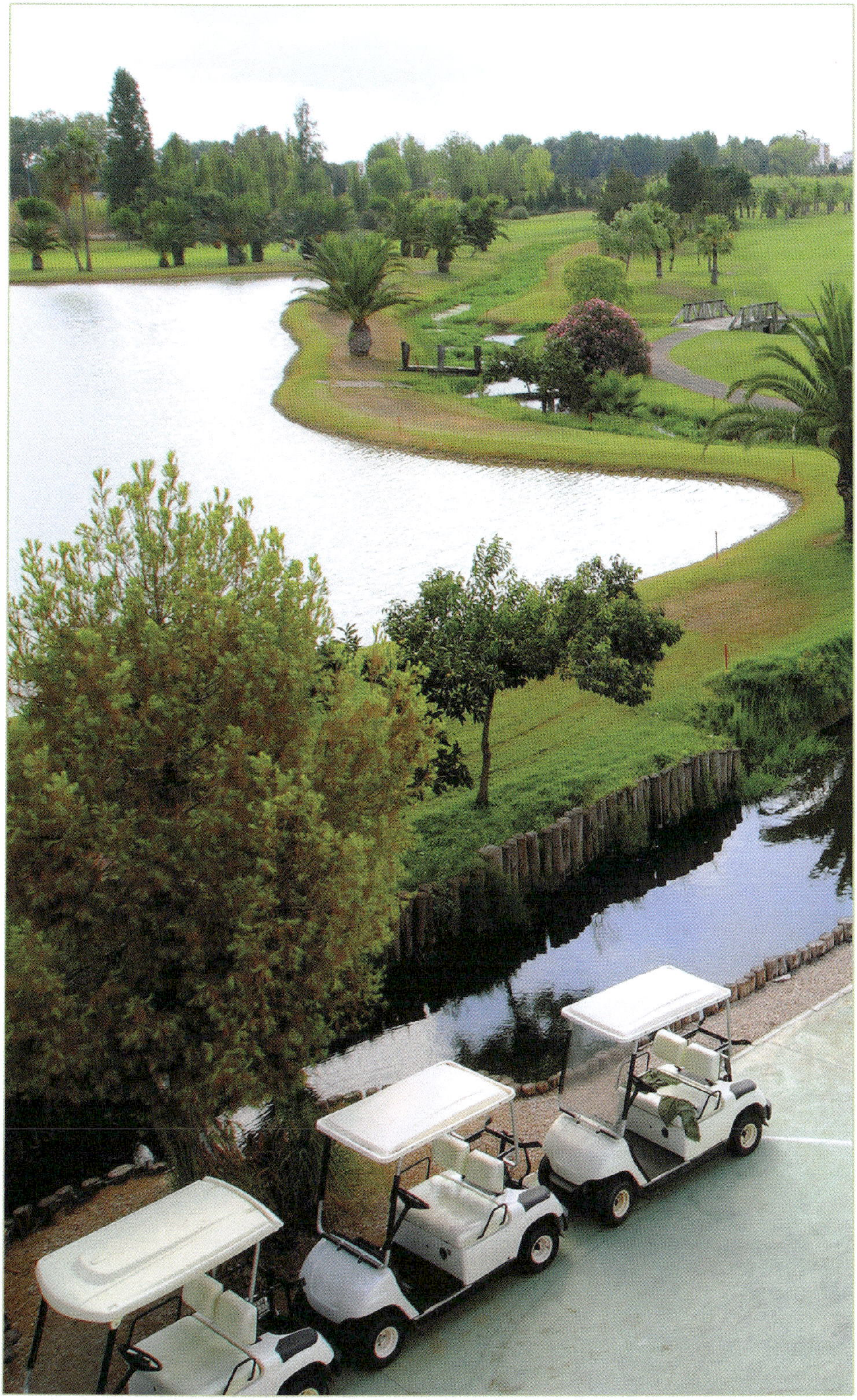

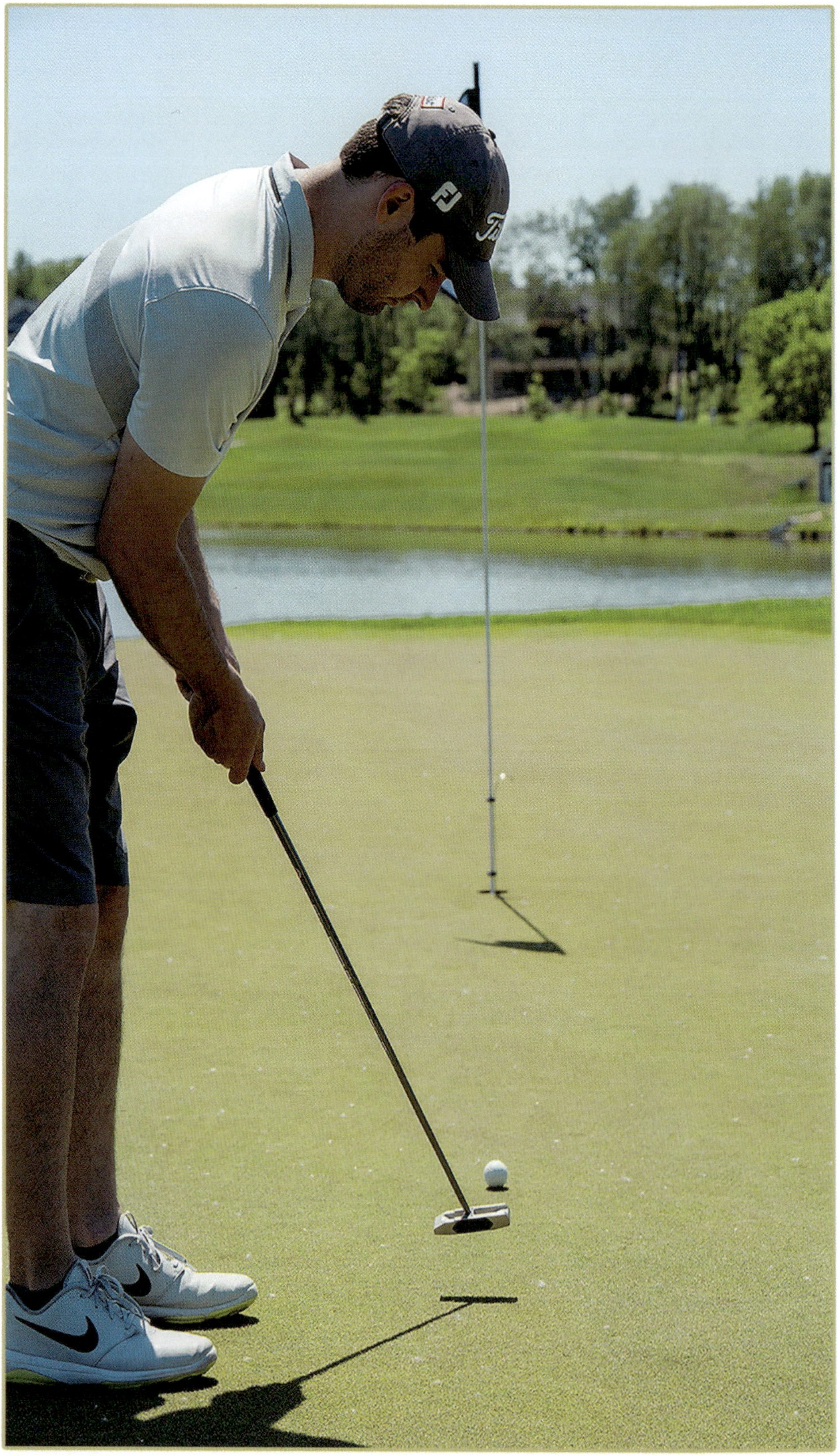

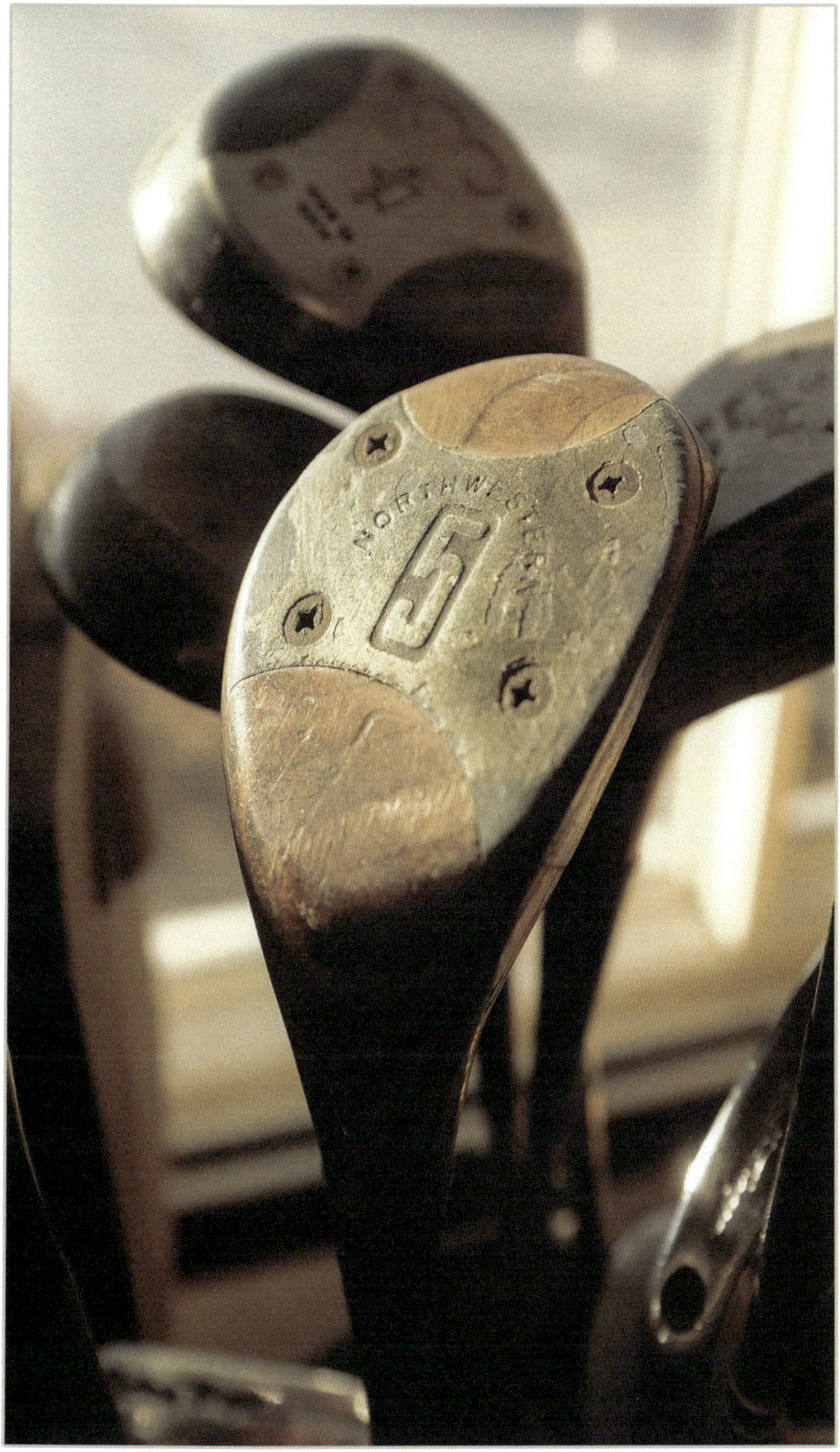
NORTHWESTERN
5

Printed in Great Britain
by Amazon

59379528R00025